VICTORY IN JESUS

LeRoy Lawson

STANDARD PUBLISHING
Cincinnati, Ohio

Library of Congress Cataloging-in-Publication Data

Lawson, E. LeRoy, 1938-
Victory in Jesus / LeRoy Lawson
    p. cm.
ISBN 0-7847-0423-6
1. Courage—Religious aspects—Christianity.   I. Title.
BV4647.C75L38   1996   95-34998
248.4—dc20   CIP

Edited by Theresa C. Hayes.
Cover design by Listenberger Design Associates.

The Standard Publishing Company, Cincinnati, Ohio.
A division of Standex International Corporation.

04   03   01   00   99   98   97   96   5   4   3   2   1

Contents

Chapter 1

For the Time of Your Life

Mark 1:14-39

Are you serious about becoming a winner in this often competitive life? Then you can't get around Lesson One: The time to get started is now. "There's no time like the present," our grandparents used to warn us. Now the media have taken over: "Today is the first day of the rest of your life." Said either way, the message is the same: "Get on with it."

It's helpful counsel. Procrastination, that popular disease, afflicts most of us. It is one of the greatest enemies of success. "I intend to get around to it—someday." "I promise you I'm going to get started on that project—tomorrow." "I'll be on it as soon as I get a couple things out of the way."

Time is so important, we had better spend a little of it as we begin this book to consider how we can best use it. As with the succeeding chapters, our approach will be to look at some scriptural principles to guide Christians to a victorious life. Since mastery of time is among our most valuable tools in developing a winning lifestyle, we start with it. The more effectively we manage our time, the more quickly we reach our life's goals.

Take advantage of *now!*

Good friends Judy and Jim Robertson served several years as missionaries in the South Pacific where they had to make many cultural adjustments. Theirs were substantial, since they moved from our desert city in the American Southwest to their steamy, verdant, laid-back home among the Samoan islanders. Their need for adjustment was not lost on their new friends. Pointing to the watch on Judy's wrist, an islander bluntly told her, "You Americans are ruled by time; we Samoans rule time."

If that's true, the Samoans are ahead of us. Ruling time is what this chapter is about. Who runs your life, you or your wristwatch? Have you, like most of your countrymen, allowed yourself to become a slave of time, your every motion dictated by calendar and schedule? It is common for Christians to boast that in Christ they have achieved mastery over sin and death; less often can we brag of taking charge of that tyrant, time.

Modern notions of time are a relatively recent invention. Certainly time existed long before clocks were invented in the twelfth and thirteenth centuries; but the arrival of clocks changed once and for all how persons would relate to it. Benedictine monks introduced clocks to the world as an aid for worship. The religious brothers observed seven periods of devotion daily; with the coming of the clock, the monks could be called to prayer at the appropriate hours. No more guesswork in their appointments for worship. As far as they were concerned, clocks served them and they used their time to serve the Lord. But not for long. What originally was employed to call believers to worship eventually was dedicated to the service of money. The clock made capitalism possible. It regulated time, standardized production, and closely monitored the workers who cranked out the goods that fueled the West's industrialization. Clock bells that once pealed for prayer time gave way to time clocks punching laborers in and out of the factory. Serving time for money soon replaced time for serving God. Today, as a matter of deplorable fact, persons rich in money complain of being bereft of time. Long ago Jesus warned that you can't serve

God and money. History has proved Him right. You'll have *time* for one or the other, but seldom for both.

Strange, isn't it, that our society has so nearly lost control of time that, when questioned, the most conscientious time server will be hard pressed to define what it is he is serving. As one philosopher asked, "Anyone with a watch can tell you what time it is, but who can tell you what is time?"[1]

"The time has come," [Jesus said.] "The kingdom of God is near. Repent and believe the good news!" (Mark 1:15).

The first chapter of Mark's Gospel seems particularly modern. Time-consciousness hurries the narrative along. Its sense of urgency compels the reader to ask, "What is this *time* that Jesus says has come?"

The Greek language is a little more helpful than English on the subject, separating our one word "time" into two. The first, *chronos,* refers to the mere passing of intervals of time. It gives us our English *chronology,* which has to do with sequence or progression, the passing of minutes or years.

The other word is *kairos,* which is time charged with meaning, as when we speak of an event's being timely, momentous or significant. *Kairos* is Jesus' word in Mark 1. The significant moment has come. Mark is careful in his Gospel, especially in this first chapter, to convince his readers that Jesus came at precisely the right time in God's plan and that He did the right (that is, God-willed) things with His time.

Give yourself to something bigger than you can handle alone

Jesus is embarking on a special quest, one of such urgency and scope He can't accomplish it alone. He has to have help, so as He launches His ministry, His first item of business is to select trustworthy companions for the mission.

> As Jesus walked beside the Sea of Galilee, he saw Simon and his brother Andrew casting a net into the lake, for they were fishermen. "Come, follow me," Jesus said, "and I will make you fishers of men." At once they left their nets and followed him.
>
> When he had gone a little farther, he saw James son of Zebedee and his brother John in a boat, preparing their nets. Without delay he called them, and they left their father Zebedee in the boat with the hired men and followed him (Mark 1:16-20).

These first four of Jesus' disciples were probably already followers of John the Baptist and knew Jesus, or at least knew enough about Him, to be receptive to His call. Notice their response, though. He charged them to become "fishers of men." He wanted their help in a mission bigger than He could handle alone, bigger than anything they had ever considered. They supplied fish for inhabitants along the northern edge of the Sea of Galilee; He wanted their help in bringing life to people everywhere.

A compelling charge. What do you think, would you have followed Him? I can hear myself. "Sorry, I'd love to, but you see, I don't have *time*. I have fish to catch, nets to repair, family duties to perform, an income to earn, meetings to attend, errands to run, chores that won't wait."

But some*times,* you have to do what you have to do, no matter what the clock says. It's a question of who is in charge, isn't it?

Do you find it as encouraging as I do that Jesus, the Son of God, recipient of the Holy Spirit (1:10), is asking for help? He does so because of the magnitude of the mission before Him. His time *(kairos)* has come, and the assignment is more than He can accomplish alone. He will have, at best, only three years. But a world and hundreds of succeeding generations are to be reached. He has to ensure the gospel work will continue after He is removed from the scene.

This first step of Jesus' ministry teaches us something about *kairos:* it cannot be contained in the moment. Anything truly significant reaches beyond itself.

Jesus' call forces the issue: Have you and I given ourselves to meaningful work that will outlast us? Jesus' ministry obviously survived His brief days on earth. We're studying His words two thousand years later. His disciples did their work well. We remember them because of Him; we remember Him because of them.

So the test: Who will remember what we are doing now after we are gone? Will our influence continue after we have left time for eternity? Or will the last shovel of dirt patted over our grave mark the end of our contribution? Everybody has the same amount of time in a day. Some invest it with long-lasting, even eternal meaning; others spend it without thought of its worth.

On a recent weekend, Cal Jernigan, our youth pastor at Central Christian, lined up five college-aged youth ministry interns in front of our worship services. They had given their summer to the church, sacrificing the season's income to work with our youth. Cal appealed to the congregation for a love offering to thank them for their good work. While he was talking about them, a pervasive sense of satisfaction filled me. I was seeing the future; these young men would carry on the ministry long after I've given it up. It was a joy to contribute to their offering. My giving was an investment in tomorrow's ministry, not totally unlike Jesus' investing himself in His disciples.

I'm getting older. My time is limited, yet my task is unfinished. Others must carry on after me. When I started nearly forty years ago, the question of who would carry on after me never entered my mind. But it entered Jesus' mind, from the very beginning. He made certain that His ministry would outlive His earthly life. Even before dispatching His disciples on their first preaching mission without Him (Matthew 10), He urged them to pray for additional workers (Matthew 9:35-38). A big job lay ahead of them. Even they wouldn't have time enough to finish the job.

Even the strongest people need friends

Something else is involved in Jesus' selection of His companions. His invitation acknowledges that even He, the Son of God, needs what we now call a support group. He needs friends. In reading the rest of Mark's Gospel, you will appreciate the depth of Jesus' love for them, His reliance on their company, His comfort in having them as prayer partners. Luke's Gospel (chapter 8) casually mentions something else, a rather obvious fact I overlooked for many years. Jesus' friends support Him financially. They make His ministry possible. He depends on them.

From the beginning He who has the power to call ten thousand angels recognizes that He is also vulnerable. He treasures his friendships. He devotes time to them.

Like all friends, His are flawed, incomplete human beings. Yet the Bible says *He* was without sin. How is friendship possible between perfection and imperfection? How can He tolerate them for so long? Can He really enjoy such blemished persons as these men turn out to be? We teach our children to be careful about the friends they select, but who could ever be good enough to fit into Jesus' company? I like to joke that I don't have a single friend who isn't flawed—and they have only one friend who is perfect. They never let me get away with it. With Jesus, though, it's no joke. He *is* the perfect friend, but He doesn't *have* any perfect ones. He can't run around with His own kind. Still, He needs friends.

The words of philosopher George Santayana often come to mind when I'm musing on the subject of friendship. He disclosed that he could find in each of his friends "a fleeting suggestion of something beautiful," and he would swear eternal friendship with that something. It was enough.

Perhaps this same principle governs Jesus in selecting His disciples. He, too, can see something beautiful in each one, some God-given quality that compensates for the imperfections. Truth to tell, they are His friends more because of His capacity to love than because of their inherent loveliness.

George Eliot picked up the following insight from some Arab sources: "A friend is one to whom one can pour out the content of one's heart, chaff and grain together, knowing that the gentlest of hands will take it and sift it and keep what's worth keeping and, with a breath of kindness, blow the rest away."

By this excellent definition, the disciples of Jesus have found a true friend. They will betray, disappoint, and desert Him, but in spite of everything, He will hold on to them. Their time together will be well spent.

Run with the right crowd!

While we can make friends at every stage of our lives, the best opportunity is when we're young, because of one advantage youth has over age: time. The time for selecting your companions is early, before the demands of career and family absorb your days. The care you give to choosing your best friends is critical, since they will help shape the rest of your days. Cementing relationships when you are older is more difficult; time is running out. You have fewer years left in which a good acquaintanceship can ripen into friendship. You don't know who your real friends are until you've been through some crises together and time has proved them faithful. The "right crowd" doesn't run out on you when you're in trouble.

A young man told me not long ago, "I haven't made any new friends lately." That's right, he hasn't. I haven't either. Few have. He has made some fine new acquaintances, though, and some of them have the potential of developing into companions—and some of them will, with the tests of time, become his friends. Among his young acquaintances and companions are some who will one day be old friends.

Please don't misunderstand me here. I am not saying that older people can't make new friends. They can and do, especially in active churches, where people of common beliefs and interests worship and work together. I'm merely stating that younger people have a natural advantage over us older adults—because time is on their side. If they are careful, if they run with the right crowd, one day they will count their assets, not in dollars and cents, but in the friends they had the good judgment to choose years earlier.

Be available for God's call
When Jesus calls the disciples, they leave what they are doing *at once* in order to follow Him. At once, *without delay.* The words read simply, but place yourself in their shoes. They are rearranging their priorities on the spot. No longer will their occupation, their families, or their co-workers dominate their lives. Jesus will. He speaks to them of the kingdom of God and their role in leading people to it, but they don't have some theological construction in mind as they walk away from their boats; they are simply following Jesus. This decision changes their lives forever.

Could I have done that? I ask myself that question every time I read this passage. Could I have turned my duties over to someone else and not looked back? And how would I have handled the issue of control? I like being in charge of my life. I don't like being told what to do. Controllers have a tough time letting someone else, even the Son of God, take over. They have difficulty saying, "Yes, Sir," when God calls them.

But there is no other right answer.

Don't forget to worship

We need to stop awhile at verse 21: "They went to Capernaum, and when the Sabbath came, Jesus went into the synagogue and began to teach."

When I was a young pastor, the religious atmosphere was charged with the anti-institutionalism of the 1960s. It was fashionable to praise Jesus and condemn formal religion. "I love Jesus, but I can't stand the church" was the popular complaint. "I don't like the institutional trappings of religion." We seemed unaware of the fact—or didn't wanted to admit—that Jesus himself participated in the institutional religion of His country. On the Sabbath He went to the synagogue. Without embarrassment He took His place as one of the leaders of worship. Since the typical first-century synagogue did not employ professional, full-time clergymen, laymen took turns in leading the singing, praying, reading and teaching the Scriptures. Jesus knew well the order of service and moved easily into the role of teacher. It seems somewhat contradictory, doesn't it, to profess to admire Jesus while disdaining something He took very seriously?

"The people were amazed at his teaching, because he taught them as one who had authority, not as the teachers of the law." My teaching and preaching make generous use of quotations and stories picked up from others. I borrow because I don't have authority. I am a teacher, one who studies and passes on to others the information he has gleaned from his research. My method is typical of preachers and teachers everywhere. But when Jesus taught, He spoke with authority. Although He was not accepted by the accredited religious leaders in Jerusalem, He had credentials they couldn't imitate, insights and knowledge of God's will, and a mind that far surpassed theirs. He didn't need to do the research that constitutes much of a modern preacher's preparation or seek anybody's approval before explaining what the Word of the Lord means. He didn't need to quote the authorities. He was and is the authority.

In our worship now, we focus on Jesus. We "fix our eyes on Jesus, the author and perfecter of our faith" (Hebrews 12:2). As we pray, praise, break bread, study God's Word and fellowship with one another, we not only acknowledge God's sovereignty in our lives but receive inspiration to continue in His service and in our growth toward Christlikeness.

I admire church people. The faithful participants in our worship every week are bombarded daily with secular, materialistic, relativistic, demonic, inane, sensual propaganda that never lets up. Yet they come to worship desiring to hear and obey the authoritative Word of the Lord. Their motives vary, but by far the majority of them are seeking an alternate opinion to the yammerings of this "crooked generation" (Deuteronomy 32:5). They have looked their society in the face and found it wanting. They want to build their lives on God's truth, not humanity's wobbling and sometimes evil untruths. They don't expect their church to be as entertaining as television; they tolerate their preacher's foibles and bear with their fellow worshipers' humanness. They have concluded the church offers something better than what their unwashed society touts as real living. They seek, as I said, a word from the Lord.

Probably the greatest nonstop source of misinformation and yes, even evil, is television. Its mesmerizing power, like nothing else in history, has taken control of people's thoughts and attitudes. For seven hours a day the average American is ingesting whatever their TVs are spewing out.

Because of this current addiction to the tube, I was fascinated to read a prediction written at the 1939 New York World's Fair. A prototype of television sets was being demonstrated. The *New York Times* sent a reviewer to learn what he could about the new phenomenon. His column didn't see much future for it. "The problem with television," he wrote, "is that the people must sit and keep their eyes glued on a screen. The average American family hasn't time for it."[2]

He was as wrong as he could be. The average American

family made time for it. My protest against television does not have much to do with this or that specific program, although there are numerous ones that should be killed. My complaint is against the watching itself, against devoting seven hours every day of a very short life span to passive viewing, to being fed what is basically intellectual, mental, spiritual pap that numbs one's conscience and perverts one's value system, that substitutes viewing for doing, watching others for developing relationships. Seven-hours-a-day people subject themselves to propaganda.

So I praise church attenders. An hour or two a week isn't much, admittedly, but for that much time at least they seek a second opinion. They ask for God's opinion on the contemporary public and personal concerns. I'm grateful for them. They take time to worship.

Invest yourself in others

When we "fix our eyes on Jesus," our eyes quickly shift to see what He sees. He looks at others who need Him. He gives himself to them. As His disciples quickly learn, to follow Jesus is to pour yourself into other lives, those with potential and those with problems. Sometimes the problems are grievous, like those of a certain demon-possessed man.

"Just then a man in their synagogue who was possessed by an evil spirit cried out, 'What do you want with us, Jesus of Nazareth? Have you come to destroy us? I know who you are—the Holy One of God!'" (Mark 1:23, 24).

Evil possesses a perverted kind of intelligence. It recognizes holiness when it sees it—and wants it dead. Wherever good is, evil is on the attack. So while others are raptly attending Jesus' teaching, this man raises a ruckus.

When the Lord speaks the truth, He elicits howls of protest from this possessed man. Evil seeks to bring truth down no matter what it takes. Notice how Jesus deals with him. His method is a bit surprising to people who believe only in the "gentle Jesus meek and mild" of the nursery. This isn't nursery talk.

"Shut up!"

The *New International Version* is a little more polite, "Be quiet!" But the force of the original text is stronger, "Come out of him!" Jesus is not addressing the man, you understand, but the evil in the man.

"The evil spirit shook the man violently and came out of him with a shriek."

Without recourse to the histrionics so popular in religious television, Jesus quietly heals the man.

"The people were all so amazed that they asked each other, 'What is this? A new teaching—and with authority! He even gives orders to evil spirits and they obey him.' News about him spread quickly over the whole region of Galilee" (vv. 27, 28).

Like wildfire it spread. "As soon as they left the synagogue, they went with James and John to the home of Simon and Andrew. Simon's mother-in-law was in bed with a fever, and they told Jesus about her. So he went to her, took her hand and helped her up. The fever left her and she began to wait on them" (vv. 29-31).

He healed her and she got up and served them. The proper response to being healed is gratitude; the logical expression of gratitude is service. When you answer Jesus' call to discipleship, you will make time to invest yourself in others if for no other reason than to express your appreciation.

Keep in close touch with the one who called you

That evening after sunset the people brought to Jesus all the sick and demon-possessed. The whole town gathered at the door, and Jesus healed many who had various diseases. He also drove out many demons, but he would not let the demons speak because they knew who he was. Very early in the morning, while it was still dark, Jesus got up, left the house and went off to a solitary place, where he prayed. Simon and his companions went to look for him, and when they found him, they exclaimed: "Everyone is looking for you!" (Mark 1:32-37).

By this time Jesus is well launched in His ministry. From now on crowds will press themselves on Him, questioning, demanding healing, never leaving Him alone. How does He keep up with the demand? Even with His disciples' help, He is nearly overwhelmed by the importuning crowd. There's no rest for the good.

He doesn't resent them. His answer is exactly the opposite of what you and I might be tempted to say to Simon Peter, "Let us go somewhere else—to the nearby villages—so I can preach there also." Wouldn't we have said, "Let's go somewhere else—to the nearby villages—so I can escape this mob and get some rest"?

"'So I can preach there also. That is why I have come.' So he traveled throughout Galilee, preaching in their synagogues and driving out demons."

The secret of His calm spirit is found in verse 35, "Jesus got up, left the house and went off to a solitary place, where he prayed."

Jesus, too, has been called to ministry. From time to time He withdraws from everybody else to seek the presence of His Father, and in His Father's presence Jesus' power is renewed so He can return to the crowds with energy. "That is why I have come." Jesus has already taken the step He has invited His disciples to take. He has "bet His life" on the mission His Father gave Him.

Chapter 2

Let the Lord
Be the Lord!

Matthew 8:5-13

In the first chapter, so much emphasis was placed on *your* control of your time that we must return to the issue of control again to be certain there is no misunderstanding. You do need to take charge of your time—but there is a preliminary step: you need to let the Lord take control of *you.* For the Christian, victory in the game of life is always victory *in Jesus.* Letting the Son be Lord is the concession the devil and his disciples could never make, as Lucifer in John Milton's *Paradise Lost* admits. Banished from Heaven by the God whom he has defied, Lucifer surveys his new home in Hell and insolently declares:

> Here at least
> We shall be free. . . .
> Here we may reign secure; and in my choice
> To reign is worth ambition, though in Hell:
> *Better to reign in Hell than serve in Heaven.*

Many of Milton's literary critics charge that he fails to "justify the ways of God to men," his stated purpose in the epic; in fact, contrary to his intention, they say he describes a Satan so attractive in his rebellion, so creative in his defiance, so winsome in his cunning that it is he, and not his divine opponent, who is the real hero of the epic. For today's readers the seventeenth-century poem aptly describes Our Man in Hell; Lucifer is our kind of guy, bravely refusing to submit to authority he doesn't like, even if it costs him Paradise. "Better to reign in Hell than serve in Heaven" is the unofficial slogan of many a modern contender. Unlike movie idol James Dean, however, they insist they are rebels *with* a cause.

W. E. Henley could have been quoting Milton's Satan in his famous "Invictus":

> Out of the night that covers me,
>   Black as the Pit from pole to pole,
> I thank whatever gods may be
>   For my unconquerable soul
> . . . .
> It matters not how strait the gate,
>   How charged with punishments the scroll,
> I am the master of my fate:
>   I am the captain of my soul.

No, you're not. When my high school English teacher encouraged our class to memorize these famous lines from Henley many years ago, I did not realize what an insidious doctrine they contain. At first blush they sound like little more than typical American can-doism, the boastful utterance of a person who will not be beaten by enemy or circumstance, who recognizes no superior, who will not bow the head to anyone or anything. They are words to be muttered at midnight, self-hypnosis to apply in a crisis.

Words strong and brave, but untrue.

Even if you are sovereign there, for all your boasting your Hell is still Hell and you can't make a heaven of it. No matter how you preen yourself, pacing the bridge in your captain's uniform, you can't still the raging storm; your fate is not yours to dictate. For all your vaunted powers, you can't turn the night into day. You can't drive away the dread disease, you can't turn death to life.

One of life's most fundamental, painful, and inescapable

lessons is learning to say with meaning, *"I am a person under authority."*

The spiritual principle we are studying in this chapter is submission. Like the old gambler in that famous country song, "You've got to know when to hold 'em [your cards] and know when to fold 'em." When you're licked, admit it. When you can't win by your own shrewdness, face it.

Recently my wife, Joy, urged me to watch a movie on eating disorders. In it an anorexic young woman of eighteen or so had nearly starved herself to death. Caught in the death grip of this deadly disease, she wanted to eat but couldn't. She picked at her food without ingesting. Her body ached; she had reduced herself to skin and bones. Her parents were baffled, desperate; they were watching their daughter die before their eyes.

Finally, in desperation, her mother convinced her father that he must sue his own daughter in court for the right to take over the decisions concerning her medical health. If the court would grant his petition, his daughter would lose all legal right to make her own eating and health decisions. The young woman was given a court-appointed attorney and appeared at the trial determined to win the right to continue to be "the master of her fate, the captain of her soul," even if it killed her. She was living in a physical Hell, but she reigned there.

In the dramatic and somewhat artificial climax, when she heard her father say he was willing to make all the decisions and take all the responsibility for her health, she capitulated. The power struggle was over. She would obey her father, she told the judge. She would acknowledge his authority.

In the brief denouement of the movie, she was shown testifying to her support group, jogging with a friend, and beaming in good health. She was no longer sovereign, but she was out of Hell.

The movie depicted a modern application of an ancient spiritual principle. The patient had to submit or she would die. "Submission" is a word not found on everybody's lips in this self-assertive age, but then, spiritual wisdom always has been more noted for its scarcity than its abundance.

The movie had a happy ending, but it left this father pondering. Had she been my daughter and had her health been placed in my hands, would I have known what to do for her? Would I have been wise enough, skilled enough, that she would have been better off under my authority than her own? I'd like to see the film again, only this time I'd like to have the director tell the story from the father's point of view. He has gained the authority. Does he have the wisdom?

My thoughts turned to another man with some authority. This one lived a long time ago, in the land of Palestine, in the days of Jesus. He was a centurion, a Roman officer in charge of one hundred soldiers. We know very little about him, only the bare facts, the most important of which are that his servant was mortally ill and that the officer had complete authority over him. What he didn't have was the knowledge or the power to help him. What he *did* have was the wisdom to turn to Someone who did. His story is found in Matthew 8:5-13:

"'Lord,' he said, 'my servant lies at home paralyzed and in terrible suffering.'

"Jesus said to him, 'I will go and heal him.'"

But that was more than the centurion was asking.

"'Lord, I do not deserve to have you come under my roof. But just say the word, and my servant will be healed.'"

His faith was exemplary in itself, but even more remarkable was his understanding of Jesus' power, a discernment he gained from his own grasp of the nature of power.

"'For I myself am a man under authority, with soldiers under me. I tell this one, "Go," and he goes; and that one, "Come," and he comes. I say to my servant, "Do this," and he does it.'"

He was accustomed to being obeyed. But this time his own authority had failed. He could not say to his servant's illness, "Begone." He needed someone with greater power to take over.

"'I tell you the truth, [Jesus said in response] I have not found anyone in Israel with such great faith.'"

Jesus defines the centurion's faith as *submission to authority.* It is a voluntary letting go of one's personal control and placing it in the hands of one more worthy to exercise it.

The end of the centurion's story can readily be guessed:

"Then Jesus said to the centurion, 'Go! It will be done just as you believed it would.' And his servant was healed at that very hour."

The officer let the Lord be the Lord—and he and his servant were the winners for it.

Let's linger with this story a little longer, because it has so much to teach about giving up the struggle in order to win it. It acts out one of Jesus' inescapable paradoxes: "For whoever wants to save his life will lose it, but whoever loses his life for me and for the gospel will save it" (Mark 8:35). Who doesn't want to save it? He makes it sound as if it is impossible to do so. Not really. It's just impossible for *us* to do so. Jesus insists that to get the most important things of life, we have to let go, resign our thrones, yield to a higher power. Like the anorexic woman, we have to quit fighting our Father and let Him help us. It's the only way to win. Who wants to lose?

A winner knows when to submit

The centurion gets right to the point with Jesus. "I know when to submit, and now is the time. You can do what I can't. Say the word." In another book I've quoted my good friend William Boice, longtime pastor of First Christian Church in Phoenix. His words bear repeating. "A good leader knows how to follow," Bill has often told me. Following was much on his mind a few years ago. He was resigning as senior minister after more than three decades at the helm of the congregation he founded. His friends all over the country wondered whether Bill could actually allow someone else to lead "his" church. "Not to worry," he assured us. "A leader knows how to follow." This former Army chaplain could give orders; he said he could obey them. And he has.

Genuine obedience is so rare among us it has given rise to many delightful stories. Perhaps my favorite is the one about the rather overbearing executive who boarded a Pullman train (this is a very old story!) leaving from New York for Chicago. He explained to the porter that he was a heavy sleeper, but "I want you to be sure and wake me at 3:00 A.M.

to get off in Buffalo. Regardless of what I say or how I fight you, get me up, for I have some important business there." Knowing the porter was in for some grief when he tried to wake him, he gave the man a large tip. The next morning, however, he was distraught when he woke up in Chicago instead of in Buffalo. He ran down the porter and excoriated him with every expletive in his arsenal of abusive language. After he stormed away, a witness asked the porter, "How could you stand there and take that kind of talk from that man?"

"That ain't nothing," the porter answered. "You should have heard what the man said that I put off in Buffalo."

The porter knew *how* to submit—he was just mistaken in knowing *whom* to obey.

We usually associate submission or obedience with the military. Civilian life in our licentious society encourages assertiveness, independence, pushing to the head of the line or to the edge of tolerance. We have long looked to the military to tame our wild youth and teach our delinquents civility. "Into the Army or into jail with them" is no idle threat.

Henry Adams, grandson of John Quincy Adams, had a gentler teacher. The former President was eighty at the time of Henry's lesson. The boy was six or seven. His mother had taken him to stay with his grandfather for the summer. Probably because it was summer, Henry stood one morning at the door in passionate rebellion against going to school. His mother, at a disadvantage because they were guests in her father-in-law's home, felt helpless against the youngster's defiance.

The disturbance took place at the foot of a long staircase at the top of which was the President's library. Suddenly the library door opened, and the old man came slowly down the steps. He put on his hat, took the boy's hand without a word, and walked with him up the road to town a mile away. Henry couldn't say a word, and his grandfather didn't. Decades later Henry wrote,

> With a certain maturity of mind, the child must have recognized that the President, though a tool of tyranny, had done his disreputable work with a certain intelligence. He had shown no temper, no

irritation, no personal feeling, and had made no display of force. Above all, he had held his tongue. During their long walk he had said nothing; he had uttered no syllable of revolting cant about the duty of obedience and the wickedness of resistance to law; he had shown no concern in the matter; hardly even a consciousness of the boy's existence. . . . For this forbearance he felt instinctive respect.[1]

As a grandfather myself, I quote Adams, marveling at the old gentleman's restraint. He took over as one having, quite simply, authority. My own grandfather had the same effect on me. My grandchildren seem less than awed by their grandpa, however. They do not submit to my will without protest. Young Henry did. It was the elder Adams's authoritative presence that squelched Henry's protest. It is a similar quality that, when we read the Gospels, causes us to stand beside the centurion and tell Jesus, "Just say the word. You have authority."

Until we accept His sovereignty, however, rebellion seems to be the order of the day.

Oswald Chambers, who is right about so many spiritual things, has noted,

God does not give us overcoming life; He gives us life *as we overcome.* When the inspiration of God comes, and He says—"Arise from the dead," we have to get up; God does not lift us up. Our Lord said to the man with the withered hand—"Stretch forth thy hand," and as soon as the man did so, his hand was healed, but he had to take the initiative."[2]

That initiative looks very much like obedience, when we acknowledge we have met more than our match. "Just say the word."

A real winner cares for the underdog

"My *servant* lies at home . . . in terrible suffering."

All right, I admit it, the centurion isn't acting totally out of his concern for his servant's life. You can say it's for his own benefit as well, and you're right. Still, there's more, don't you think?

Do you believe this centurion, so accustomed to being in control, finds it easy to ask for help? Don't you think this Roman, this member of the army of the occupation, this official of the conquering empire charged with protecting peace and order in the fractious, cranky conquered nation, had to struggle with his racial prejudice to become convinced he should humble himself before this member of the occupied nation? I can't imagine his submitting to Jesus for himself, can you? He does it because he's desperate on behalf of another, one who can't do for himself and for whom he, the man with authority, can do nothing. There's an element of nobility in him.

One of the most appealing vignettes in Peggy Noonan's biography of Ronald Reagan describes a scene in the bathroom adjoining the President's hospital room. John Hinckley's assassination attempt had not been fatal, but the bullet wound was serious enough to hospitalize Mr. Reagan. The still-weakened President had spilled some water and was on his hands and knees cleaning up after himself so that, he explained to his surprised aides, a nurse wouldn't have to. He didn't want to bother her with the problem he'd caused. His presidency will long be a controversial one, but that one small incident goes a long way toward explaining how Ronald Reagan, ex-lifeguard, ex-actor, ex-television host became one of America's most popular Presidents. There was an element of nobility in this head of state. He could humble himself.

So could the centurion. The Bible says Jesus marveled over the man's faith. It does not say, but I suspect it's true, that an instant rapport was established between the compassionate Healer and the servant's concerned lord. The centurion was abasing himself for the sake of his subordinate. He was doing what the Savior often taught. One thinks of the parable of the good Samaritan (Luke 10), or the parable of the sheep and the goats (Matthew 25), in which Jesus identifies himself with the lowest of humanity: "I tell you the truth, whatever you did for one of the least of these brothers of mine, you did for me." In Jesus' world, the real winners take care of the underdogs.

A real winner doesn't require the spectacular

The subheading should be stronger, perhaps. Real winners not only don't require the spectacular, they are suspicious of it. "Just say the word, and my servant will be healed," the centurion tells Jesus. He doesn't require special consideration and doesn't ask for spectacle. It isn't "Show time in Capernaum" for him.

Pardon me if that paragraph sounds a little cynical. During the past few years, America has seen too much emphasis on the spectacular, even in evangelical Christianity. The gullible have been gulled. The skeptic has had his skepticism justified. It isn't just the television scandals I'm referring to, but the ongoing, successful religious shows that imitate Hollywood at its glitziest.

The centurion doesn't ask for razzmatazz and Jesus doesn't perform it. But then, Jesus regularly refrains from showmanship. He rejects the devil's temptation to dazzle the crowds by casting himself from the pinnacle of the temple (Matthew 4:5, 7). He dismisses the crowd before raising the little girl from her deathbed (Mark 5:40). He cautions those whom He helps to be quiet about what He has done. When He is transfigured and appears with Moses and Elijah, only His closest friends are with Him. He never appears in the pages of Scripture as a man in search of publicity. Another reason for the rapport of centurion and Savior, then, is this respect each has for quiet authenticity.

A much, much later follower of Jesus, Mother Teresa of India, reminds those who inquire after her secret of success, "God calls us to *faithfulness, not success.*" Hers is a good reminder to harried Christian leaders caught up in today's success syndrome. When pastors meet, it isn't long before they're sharing their statistics: who has the largest membership, biggest attendance, most additions, most successful recent special event, and so on. Others boast of their sensational gifts, calling attention to their speaking in tongues, recounting the miraculous healings taking place in their churches, or swaggering about the new building program with the largest ever recreational hall, or whatever.

Recently Christian Burleson Borrmann sang at John and Sherry Chandler's wedding. Christian has one of the finest contralto voices I've heard. When she sang "How Beautiful," she held her audience spellbound. Yet she had no backup band, no taped accompaniment that the audience could hear. She trusted her own voice to convey the beautiful message. She wore no flashy costume and exhibited no practiced gestures. Just quality music, sung with authority. A simple song, sung with elegant simplicity.

That's the essence of accomplishment in any field, isn't it? Don't we say of the gifted athlete, "He makes it look so easy"? Doesn't the gifted musician amaze us with the apparent ease of execution, especially when we pick up the instrument ourselves?

On the other hand, what do we say of the inept performer? He made a *spectacle* of himself, didn't he?

To be a winner, trust is the essential
"I have not found anyone in Israel with such great faith."
". . . subjects of the kingdom will be thrown outside"

As a staunch Christian, you may have concluded by now that this chapter is really saying, "Just let go and let God." In a sense, that's right. But the saying is easier spoken than applied. Are these words just a tired cliché or are they really good spiritual advice? For that matter, what do they mean? Let go of what? Let God do what? Why, if the saying is such good counsel, does it always seem to be offered by the most passive, even the most unsuccessful people you know? And why is this advice usually aimed at the least passive, usually more successful "take-charge types," sometimes more critically called, the "controllers"?

Are you in financial trouble? "Let go and let God."

Are you worrying about your children because they have fallen in with bad company? "Let go and let God."

Is your health troubling you? "Let go and let God."

Easy for *you* to say, perhaps, but not easy for me to do. Trust does not come easy to people accustomed to being in charge. Believers like me, for whom submission does not come naturally, are not helped very much by "easy-believers." Perhaps that is why the centurion is so appealing to us. We can identify with the obstacles he must have overcome before placing his faith in Jesus.

German theologian Hans Küng, speaks to the likes of the

centurion and me. He writes of faith as, "an act of the human being as a whole . . . or, more precisely, an act of reasonable trust for which there may be no strict proofs, but for which there are good reasons."

Küng speaks to the challenge of modern belief. Since proof of Jesus' divine authority rests on scriptural testimony, and since that testimony has been debated by so many for so long, how can a person, especially one who prides himself on basing his decisions on "just the facts, ma'am" (to quote the realist Jack Webb in *Dragnet),* trust either Jesus or the Scriptures? Küng recognizes the difficulty. For such a person faith is, "like committing oneself to someone else in love after some doubts; strictly speaking one has no strict proofs for this trust, but one does have good reasons—as long as this is not a fatal 'blind love.' And blind faith can have as devastating consequences as blind love."

Küng isn't appealing for blind faith but for reasonable trust. He reminds us that Augustine of Hippo, the great teacher of the Latin church, already made a distinction: it is not just a matter of "believing something" *(credere aliquid), or* even of "believing someone" *(credere alicui),* but of "believing in someone" *(credere in aliquem).* That is the meaning of the primal word *credo,* "I believe."[3]

His appeal takes us back to the centurion who, in spite of all reservations he could reasonably be expected to entertain, trusted *in* Jesus.

Corrie ten Boom is as different a believer from the scholarly Küng as she can be, yet she comes to a similar conclusion. Faith, she says, is a

Fantastic
   Adventure
     In
       Trusting
      Him

Her text is Psalm 37:5, "Commit your way to the Lord; trust in him, and he will act."[4]

It is a good text for us as well, isn't it?

In this chapter we've used several words which form a cluster of meanings, each one enhancing the meaning of the others, all of them together defining the faith that wins. To have faith in Jesus, then, is to submit, to obey, to commit, to remain faithful, to trust.

A person of faith is a person *under authority.*

Chapter 3

Why Love
Is Not Enough

John 4:1-42

When our twenty-six-year-old son took his life, he left behind a five-page letter designed to ease the pain of his family and other loved ones. "I've got a lot to say," he told us. He was writing "to answer as many of the possible questions as I can." He wanted to help us through "the inevitable questioning period that follows this sort of thing." He wrote lovingly of his family, his reasons for what seemed to us his inexplicable suicide, his logic in selecting the campground where he did it, and his desires for the disposition of his tiny estate.

It was a good letter, if there is such a thing as a good suicide note, but it failed to answer all the questions. One especially haunted his father, the one about love. If ever a person loved and was loved, it was Lane. For weeks, for example, his mother had been planning to travel from Arizona to Oregon for an extended visit with Lane. When she talked with him on the phone that week, she accelerated her plans, hearing the discouragement in his voice. She was to have left just four days after we received word of his death.

As soon as we could make flight arrangements for Oregon, we began trying to contact his grandparents in Salem. They weren't home. Joy's brother and sister-in-law helped us, and we finally located them attending a fiftieth anniversary celebration for friends in Florence. They were about to leave for Brookings, where they planned to spend some time with Lane. With all of us—his grandparents, his parents, his sisters, his nephews—Lane was a favorite. Whenever possible he came home for extended visits. He was the first to arrive for holidays, and the last to leave. He had no doubt about the love of his family, and his family never doubted his love for us.

In addition, Lane was socially popular and could boast, though he never did, of many friends who sincerely loved him and would do anything he asked of them. At his memorial services, recent and longtime friends attended and shared with his family their love for him. And in his letter he spoke glowingly of the new love of his life. We met Diane and saw immediately why he fell for her. She appeared to be just the kind of woman he needed, one with whom he could have spent a long and fruitful life.

Hence the question that would not go away. He was loved, he was loving.

But love isn't enough, is it?

Two Scriptures helped me find the inescapable answer to my question. The first is the great commandment, "Love the Lord your God with all your heart and with all your soul and with all your mind. . . . Love your neighbor as yourself" (Matthew 22:37-39).

Lane had lived the second half of the commandment. He loved his neighbors, and he defined "neighbor" generously. The testimonies were universal: others saw him as we saw him, a kind, considerate, giving, compassionate human being. He received the ultimate compliment when at the memorial services his "adopted" brother Brian chose to read Jesus' Beatitudes because, he said, they described Lane: a lover.

He also loved God, although he would probably, at this searching stage of his maturation, have substituted truth or reality or some other more abstract, less personal (and loaded) word than God. It was here, as a matter of fact, that his strength faltered. Like many thinkers, Lane was searching for a god somewhat different, one that would distinguish his faith from that of his father and mother. An inherited religion wasn't for him. He wanted to make his own way, do his own thing, find his own god. Having let go of his parents' God and having not yet firmly grasped or been grasped by any other, he fell. What we call a sustaining faith eluded him. That hope against hope wasn't his. When the immediate pain grew too great, he had no confidence in a future better than today, in a providence that would pull him through, in a destiny worth enduring the present.

The second Scripture concludes one of the Bible's greatest chapters, 1 Corinthians 13, the "love chapter." Embedded in Paul's incomparable discussion of proper worship, this chapter elevates love as the most excellent way to adore God. Spiritual gifts are marvelous aids to worship, particularly when they build up the whole body of Christ, but they gain real efficacy only when they are exercised for loving purposes and in a loving manner. Hence Paul's hymn to love.

After praising and describing this greatest of human attributes, speaking of the everlastingness of love and the maturation of the lover, he abruptly introduces two other elements, which he neither praises nor describes but which, it seems, he dare not leave out. *"And now these three remain: faith, hope and love. But the greatest of these is love."*

Paul often speaks of this trinity, as if in his thinking you can't ever have one without the other two.

Never before Lane's suicide had I taken Paul's words so seriously. In spite of love's magnificence, in spite of love's efficacy as the means of proper worship, in spite of its preeminence over faith and hope, we must not be misled: faith and hope also remain. Love without faith and hope is desperately incomplete.

Lane and I often spoke about God. He was most respectful, as evidenced in his embracing of Jesus' ethical teaching, but he did not appreciate all the religious trappings of Christianity. He had not yet separated the chaff of religiosity from the wheat of Christian faith. Frederick Buechner, in his *Magnificent Defeat,* could have been describing Lane: "Each of us . . . carries around inside himself, I believe, a certain emptiness—a sense that something is missing, a restlessness, a deep feeling that somehow all is not right inside his skin. Psychologists sometimes call it anxiety, theologians sometimes call it estrangement. . . ."[1]

What is so devastating about this love that does not believe and thus despairs of hope is that when the pain is too great, love by itself can't save the lover's life.

Lane, with his decidedly philosophical mind, would not have disputed Alexis de Tocqueville's observation, "There is no philosopher in the world so great but he believes a million things on the faith of other people and accepts a great many more truths than he demonstrates."[2]

Lane hadn't fallen into the empiricists' trap of believing that only the observable, repeatable, and verifiable are real. He did not make his own sensate experiences the acid test of what is believable and what is not. He just was not persuaded that his religious forebears, including his father and mother, had all the truth wrapped up in their creeds and rites. His father liked to reflect on George Santayana's saying, "We cannot know who first discovered water. But we can be sure that it was not the fish."[3] Lane undoubtedly saw his parents as pretty much like the fish, content to swim in currents Someone Else has provided, without having to know precisely Who put them there or even how they can know Who did it or why it's necessary to know. He, on the other hand, doggedly sought answers and, until he found them, he could love but he couldn't wholeheartedly believe and, when faith faltered, hope fled. Love wasn't enough.

His parents had prayed that God would protect all their children until they could grow through the painful questioning years, until their loving natures could enjoy the harmony of love, faith and hope. In Lane's case, that was not to be.

Jesus once met a woman who was apparently ready to believe. She was already an expert in love, or at least some form of love. John's Gospel gives us only cryptic glimpses of her personal life. The facts are baldly stated; the turbulence behind the facts are left to be grasped by the sensitive reader.

Five husbands she had had and she wasn't legally married to the man with whom she was currently living. She went to the well in Sychar to draw water "about the sixth hour," as if she wanted to avoid the crowd that would have been there earlier, when the more respectable women in town would be getting their day's supply. Somewhere in the back of my mind is a fragment of a conversation with a movie star who offered her opinion regarding marriage, then added with some force, "I know what I'm talking about. After all, I've been married five times!" No thinking person would accept a person married that many times as an expert on marital love. On lust, maybe, or infatuation or cohabitation or serial polygamy. But not on love.

In a similar sense, perhaps, we would grant that the woman at the well was experienced in love of a type. But she, too, found it inadequate. Otherwise, would she have so quickly, once she sensed Jesus' prophetic insight, turned the conversation to matters of faith and hope? "I can see that you are a prophet. Our fathers worshiped on this mountain, but you Jews claim that the place where we must worship is in Jerusalem."

"Where," she is asking, "can I find God?" Samaritans knew where: on Mt. Gerizim, "this mountain." Jews knew where: "In Jerusalem." She is astute enough to know that both answers can't be correct, and hungry enough to seek the truth from this Prophet, even though He is a Jew.

Jesus does not minimize the difference. He even claims superiority for the Jewish traditions ("You Samaritans worship what you do not know; we worship what we do know, for salvation is from the Jews"), yet He goes on to state that though the Jews *have been* correct until now, a new era is being introduced ("a time is coming and has now come") that challenges the Jews' historic understanding. Religion is taking a new form, demanding a new expression.

"God is spirit, and his worshipers must worship in spirit and in truth."

Such worship has little to do with mountains and temples and formalized rituals, and much to do with truth found through love and faith and hope.

On a recent tour to the Holy Land, we fellow travelers were commenting on the many kinds of religions we were studying. We were surrounded by the varieties of Judaism, of course, running the spectrum from the super orthodox in their black clothes and ringlets to the secular, completely this-worldly Jews. A visit to the Church of the Holy Sepulchre introduces the visitor to five separate denominations of Christianity, all different from the evangelical faith of our tour group members. Not far away we visited the Dome of the Rock, a special shrine for members of Islam, the Muslim faith. After leaving Palestine our group spent several days in Greece where we immersed ourselves in the ruins depicting ancient Greek paganism—and saw no little evidence of its contemporary incarnation. In the course of a few short days we couldn't escape coming to several conclusions:

1) For all our talk of this being a "secular" era, religion has played and is continuing to play a supremely significant role in human affairs.

2) Every religion speaks of the spiritual, but makes generous use of the physical to glorify God.

3) Proponents of each of these faiths are convinced that theirs is the true religion and all of the others are in error.

4) To conclude that all roads lead to God, as certain world religions teach, requires a type of intellectual gymnastics beyond the ability of most thinkers, and to say that every religion is as good as every other religion is to have given up thought altogether.

5) If there is a God (or gods), He (or they) cannot be limited to Jerusalem or Mt. Gerizim. God must be spirit.

Georges Bernanos' narrator in his *Diary of a Country Priest* is a poverty-stricken *cure,* a notably unsuccessful priest even in his own eyes. He is dying of cancer. With death imminent, he learns that it is not going to be possible for him to receive extreme unction, Roman Catholicism's final sacrament. Told that no priest can arrive in time to administer the sacrament to him, he remarks in words bordering on the scandalous, "Does it matter?" It doesn't, he says, because *"Tout est grace"* ("All is grace"). Bernanos' English translator renders it beautifully, "Grace is everywhere."[4]

Grace isn't the possession solely of Jerusalem or Mt. Gerizim, the Jews or the Samaritans. Grace is of God, available wherever His Spirit ministers. Grace, which is God's expression of love, moves beyond love's borders. It is available wherever God is and, since God is spirit, it is not confined by geography or chronology. Grace has provided the evidence that God is, that God loves, that God saves, that God desires those whom He loves to come to Him. Grace lifts tired eyes from earth's discouraging trials to a future of hope because of a Savior in whom one can have faith. When love falters, then, grace provides reason for hope and faith to hang on.

"My food," said Jesus, "is to do the will of him who sent me and to finish his work" (John 4:34)

Jesus' disciples couldn't understand the behavior of this holy man talking in public with a woman of soiled reputation. They didn't dare question Him; their approach was more subtle, indirect: "Rabbi, eat something."

"I have food to eat that you know nothing about."

Could someone have brought Him food, they wondered. What was He talking about?

His subject was still the worship of God, only in a more immediate, physical context. The woman was concerned about the proper way to serve God; the disciples failed to see that serving God was precisely what Jesus was doing as He discussed these theological issues with this woman, a person the more proper followers of Jesus would have shunned. Food they understood; faith in its fullness still eluded them.

For the woman, love wasn't enough. She'd tried it. For Jesus, food wasn't, either. "My food," Jesus explained, "is obedience to my Father." He was speaking the language of faith. What sustained Him was not just love, their love for Him, His for them. He had a higher calling, a duty beyond the moment. For that duty He could sacrifice food, approval, anything. Because of His singleness of purpose, the writer of Hebrews urges us to "fix our eyes on Jesus, the author and perfecter of our faith, who for the joy set before him endured the cross, scorning its shame (12:2).

Jesus, the great example in so many other ways, is also our mentor in the meaning of faith. His faith guides His decisions, leads Him into His future. While we often speak of "losing our faith," the truth is we do not so much lose it as abuse it, sapping it of its influence. We don't misplace it; we just stop letting it shape our lives, color our decisions, dictate our future.

Dr. Diane Komp, a pediatrician specializing in the care of children with cancer, returned to belief in God after a difficult struggle. She learned from her clinical mentor to keep her feelings about her patients as much under control as possible, until she felt herself going numb. Her strict regimen had the side effect of causing her faith, once so vital, to slip farther away with the passing of each child. In retrospect she concluded that few people experience a dramatic conversion from faith to disbelief; rather, "faith dies from disuse atrophy, a failure to be exercised."[5] It ceases to be food for the soul. It slips away and takes hope with it, leaving only, in the case of good people, love. And love isn't enough.

It was not so with Jesus. He kept His eye on the joy set before Him, refusing to be deflected from His course. His mission was like food and drink to Him; nothing sustained Him like His consciousness of His Father's will for Him.

After her conversation with Jesus, the transformation in this Samaritan woman is remarkable. She who came to the well at an odd hour in order to avoid the other women there now goes boldly back into town, buttonholing everybody she meets. "Come, see a man who told me everything I ever did." She not only tells of their conversation, but she even speculates, "Could this be the Christ?" Their curiosity piqued, they go to see for themselves. John reports that many of them now believed, and not just because of her testimony but, as they say, "We have heard for ourselves, and we know that this man really is the Savior of the world."

Elton Trueblood comments that, "the greatest vitality of the Christian community is found among persons who, though they do not claim to know very much, affirm that they believe Christ was right. A Christian is a person who bets his life that this is really so."[6] John's purpose for including this encounter in his Gospel is to offer further proof that, "Jesus is the Christ, the Son of God, and that by believing you may have life in his name" (20:31).

My purpose for retelling the story here is to underscore the importance of faith and hope in concert with love.

At our son's memorial services, as with so many others over the years, I read Psalm 23. "The Lord is my shepherd. . . ." These verses are the ones most quoted on such occasions. They speak of a childlike faith, an unquestioning trust in the goodness of God who, like a shepherd, cares for His own.

I did not read the 22nd Psalm, though I felt like it. If Psalm 23 speaks of a childlike faith, Psalm 22, ascribed to David, speaks of faith which holds on "in spite of."

"My God, my God, why have you forsaken me? Why are you so far from saving me, so far from the words of my groaning?"

David does not deny God's existence or even his benevolent care of the nation of Israel:

"Yet you are enthroned as the Holy One; you are the praise of Israel. In you our fathers put their trust; . . . they trusted and were not disappointed."

Yet the deliverance Israel experienced at God's hand eludes him. He cries aloud day and night, but gets no answer. He is plunged into despair:

"But I am a worm and not a man, scorned by men and despised by the people. All who see me mock me; they hurl insults, shaking their heads."

His condition is deplorable:

"I am poured out like water, and all my bones are out of joint. My heart has turned to wax; it has melted away within me. My strength is dried up like a potsherd, and my tongue sticks to the roof of my mouth; you lay me in the dust of death."

Throughout his lamentation, though, the reader detects the inescapable note of faith. David believes, in spite of. God seems to have abandoned him, even to have singled him out for special suffering, yet the psalmist will not take the fatal step of denying God's power or existence. Instead, the final verses turn to praise:

"For he has not despised or disdained the suffering of the afflicted one; he has not hidden his face from him but has listened to his cry for help."

Something has happened. In the depths of his pain, he remembers. God has been with him, and He will be. To use Peter Berger's word, he remembers "the ultimate benignness of the universe," which Berger describes as a sense that the "transcendent reality I have perceived is not only out but is there for *me.*"[7]

I have not been abandoned, God has not forsaken me. I believe. I hope in Him.

Psalm 22 has a happy ending. A particularly gripping modern parable doesn't. It's about a twelve- or thirteen-year-old boy crazed by anger or depression. He got hold of a gun and killed his father. When the authorities asked the boy why he did it, he told them he couldn't stand his father, who had always demanded too much of him, getting after him for this or that. He hated his father, he said. Later on, after he had been locked up in a house of detention, a guard walking the corridors late one night heard sounds from the boy's room. He stopped to listen. "I want my father, I want my father," he heard the youngster sobbing. Frederick Buechner labels the story "a kind of parable of the lives of all of us," with modern society very much like that boy in the house of detention. As a society we have killed our Father. God is hardly taken seriously anymore by sophisticated opinion makers. We've outgrown Him and won't put up with His demands any longer. The faith that once informed our country does so no longer. Unanswered questions have replaced traditional convictions.[8]

Instead of the faith of our fathers and the hope of this once hopeful land, today's pundits and celebrities praise love, and love alone. It's the one unassailable value in this cynical era. But as we learned at our house, love isn't enough. To achieve victory in the struggle for life, faith, hope, and love must abide, all three, even if the greatest of these is love.

Chapter 4

The Great Breakthrough: Gratitude

Luke 17:11-19

In the comforting flood of cards and letters we received during the weeks following Lane's death, one was totally unanticipated. It came from Jim and Emma Wilkins. Eleven years earlier the Wilkinses' son had committed suicide. We did not know him well, but his sister Priscilla had been my student at Milligan College, and she and her husband Tim served a year's internship on our ministerial staff in Indianapolis. They were not only former students and fellow ministers, but good friends. However, we were half a continent apart when the awful news of young Jim's suicide came to us. Our hearts ached for Priscilla and her godly parents. We didn't know what to write, how to offer comfort. "How sorry we were to receive your letter with the sad news of Jim's death! I know there aren't any words by which we could express our sympathy or understanding." With such innocuous words I began our letter.

"You did not mention how your parents are doing," I wrote in a later paragraph. "That must have been an almost unbearable shock to them also. I can't imagine losing one of my children."

I was writing my letter while still coming to terms with the loss of my father several months earlier. Priscilla had mentioned what a comfort her own son Jonathan was to her, somewhat filling the hole where Jim used to be. I identified with her feelings. "As early as the day of Dad's memorial service, I realized how deeply I felt about our son, Lane; the two closest males in my life were my father and my son. I hope that I have not been overbearing as I sense myself almost forcing my affection on Lane. I'm hoping he understands."

He did. Now that he is gone, I don't have to imagine losing one of my children. I know how it feels.

The reason I can quote the letter so accurately is that Priscilla's parents did something totally unexpected, something extremely helpful. The envelope bearing the letter from Jim and Emma Wilkins enclosed a copy of my 1983 letter to them. In the depths of our mourning, they encouraged us to read the words we had sent their daughter eleven years earlier. It was difficult to read some of the parts quoted above. The final paragraphs, though, express the way I felt in 1983—and still felt in 1995:

"I believe with increasing fervor that there is a spiritual comfort which we realize in Christ that sustains us in times like this. No quick answers, no easy explanations, no avoidance tricks, but a sustaining presence and a deepening compassion do seem to come to us from above.

"There is also the hope that is based upon the mercy and insight of a God who knows the hidden parts of the heart as we never can, and who is quicker to forgive than to judge. I have come, in times like these, to thank God for God, especially for the fact that His wisdom is not limited, nor is His mercy strained."

The key to Joy's recovery and mine is found in that last sentence: We have come, "in times like these, to thank God for God." In that thanksgiving is victory.

Weeks after receiving the Wilkinses' letter, dear friend Dolly Chitwood sent a brief note from India: "Dear Roy and Joy, I ran across this the other day and felt that I must send it on to you, praying that our loving Father has already blessed you with such peace." She had typed out a little poem entitled, "Peace after Sorrow." Nothing else we received quite so accurately verbalizes the inner serenity that now accompanies our days.

Peace After Sorrow

There is a peace which comes after sorrow
    A peace of hope surrendered, not fulfilled;
A peace that looks not upon tomorrow
    But backward, on the storm already stilled.
It is the peace in sacrifice secluded,
    The peace that is from inward conflict free;
Tis not the peace which over Eden brooded
    But that which triumphed in Gethsemane.

Gethsemane's peace still had to deal with outward conflict and ultimate death, but in the garden Jesus uttered his resolute "Yet not as I will, but as you will." For Him, too, God was God; He trusted His Father's mercy and love.

Some other good friends, Bill and Kay Tennison, also wrote us. We had been anticipating their letter, because just two years earlier they had lost their sixteen-year-old Stephanie in a freak automobile accident. Although I presided over her memorial service, the Tennisons ministered to all who came to offer condolences. Their gracious strength was an inspiration then. We wanted to hear what they had to say to us now.

Kay wrote, "The loss of a child is one of life's supreme tests. Nothing I can say will take away the pain. It will continue to come and go; however, the chasms between the waves of despair will begin to subside. . . .

"I'm so glad that God blessed us with Stephanie and that we have sixteen years of wonderful memories to draw upon. You must feel the same about your son."

We do. Bill's words were equally helpful: "The older I become, the more I come to realize what a fragile hold we have on those parts of our life which we love. It seems to me that God puts us together only for a while then we must go on our way. I am very thankful that God has chosen to put you in our lives."

They invited us to spend several days of quiet recuperation with them in their mountain retreat in Colorado. The invitation included a typically generous offer of airline tickets.

In both letters, there is thanksgiving. Their quiet strength is drawn from hearts that take seriously the apostle Paul's injunction in 1 Thessalonians 5:18. They "give thanks in all circumstances, for this is God's will for you in Christ Jesus," even in the most dreaded of all circumstances.

May I share one last letter from a parent? In this case, not from one who has lost a child, but who herself was nearly lost. In our congregation is a quiet believer whose story we had never heard until she wrote to comfort us. Her story is more dramatic, but her conclusion is the same. She writes:

> On July 5, 1978, I was taking Christopher, our son, to swim team practice where we lived in Illinois. As I rounded a curve, the pickup truck that was coming ran straight into the door on my side of the car instead of making the curve. Christopher was fine except for a sore knee and I was in and out of consciousness, so I was able to see that he was OK. Before the accident, I was in great physical shape and playing a lot of tennis. After the accident, I had a punctured lung, broken ribs and broken left arm which was cut badly and I lost a lot of blood. I was having great difficulty breathing. Although this was a bad experience in many ways, it was also rewarding.
>
> A man that was working along the road saw the entire incident. He got in the car with me, I was not able to move and never saw him, I only heard him. He assured me that Christopher was fine, he covered me with a swim towel and when I was conscious continually asked me if I was saved and knew the Lord. I do believe in angels. No one got his name or knew who he was, but said he had come to the hospital to check on me numerous times. I was never able to thank him although he has been one of the most important people in my life and he will always be remembered in my prayers.

She confesses she isn't sure "why God spoke to me in this way, but I am thankful for the experience and even though my left arm is now deformed I understand that the body is only a shell."

There's that word again: *thankful*. For all of us who have been traumatized by death in one of its many guises, life can never again be quite what it was before. We have been changed, some to become more fearful, or bitter, or vengeful, or morose. Others, who have felt the touch of God in the darkness, come to gratitude. Sometimes suddenly, other times gradually, peace encompasses them, a peace not based on explanations but on exaltation, on the perception that through it all and in it all God has been quietly bringing good out of evil (see Romans 8:28). The only appropriate response is to say thanks.

This seems so predictable a conclusion I almost hesitate to write it. Yet it isn't. I have quoted portions of letters from believers who have triumphed over the ravages of death, who have received mercy at the hand of the Lord and returned to express appreciation. Not everyone does so, though. Consider that famous incident in which Jesus healed the ten lepers—and only one said, "Thank you." Does the ratio surprise you?

The grateful one, Luke carefully points out in his narrative of the incident, was a Samaritan. Is Luke surprised that he isn't one of Jesus' countrymen—or is his purpose for mentioning race another way of reminding us that a prophet is not without honor except among his own kind? Perhaps there's something else at work here, the not untypical assumption on the part of the other nine that they somehow deserved, whereas the Samaritan, not of Jesus' people, knew he didn't, and thus was all the more grateful. At any rate, because of his gratitude, he was the one to whom Jesus said with some finality, "Your faith has made you well."

Faith, or gratitude? Is there much of a difference, in the final analysis? Have you noticed that the longer you walk with the Lord, the less you ask of Him and the more you thank Him? Thanksgiving is acknowledging a debt, admitting one is not self-sufficient, appreciating that one receives so much more in this life than one either deserves or can provide for oneself. It is, finally, a lifestyle, a far-seeing perspective on reality. It is the great philosophical breakthrough, when one sees one's actual role (which is infinitesimally small) in the running of the universe and is simply glad to be alive, to be the recipient of largesse not of one's own making or design. Thanksgiving drives out bitterness and protest, exposes demanding personalities as the ridiculous ingrates they are. A grateful heart is a wholesome heart. It has been made well.

In chapter two we saw the President of the United States on his hands and knees in his hospital bathroom, performing the work of a servant. As a young man, Ronald Reagan worked for several years as a swimming pool lifeguard. He gained an unforgettable insight into humanity in that role. In a 1941 interview in Hollywood, he commented on the lack of gratitude he received for his efforts. He counted seventy-seven lives he had saved in his six years on the job. Of that large number, only one person—a blind man—ever thanked him for saving his life. Reagan's numbers were even more discouraging than Jesus'.

A reporter asked Mr. Reagan to explain why so few gave thanks. "I believe it's a combination of embarrassment and pride," he answered. "Almost invariably they either argued they weren't in any trouble or were so mad at themselves they wouldn't admit someone else had succeeded where they had failed."[1]

Embarrassment and pride. A deadly alliance. "How could this happen to *me?*" Or, "Actually, it didn't happen as you think it did. This isn't what it looks like." How much easier to say, "Yes, it happened, and I'm a little embarrassed about it, but even more I am grateful to the one who pulled me out."

When your son dies at his own hand, you feel the pangs of embarrassment and pride. Try as you might, explain his illness as many times as you feel the need to, you can't help believing that if only you had been a better parent, this tragedy would not have happened. Your son was an adult, you tell yourself. He made his own choices, he reassured you of his love in doing so, he demanded the right to do what he felt was best, even though you are convinced he was wrong. You really couldn't have stopped him. Or could you? How do you explain him to the world? What words do you use to cover your own blushing, to keep your self-respect? How do you keep from drowning in your own self-pity?

Try giving thanks. Gratitude is healthier. No excuses, no explanations, no protestations of innocence. Simple thanksgiving to the One who saves, and for the one you've lost. We become like the intellectually troubled young G. K.

Chesterton, who confessed he finally "hung on to religion by one thin thread of thanks."

An Old Testament precedent for Chesterton's "thin thread of thanks" is Daniel's response to palace intrigue that threatened his life. The able, incorruptible administrator pleased his monarch but infuriated his fellow courtiers. The Persian King Darius recognized the exceptional ability of his Jewish administrator and planned to make him prime minister over the whole kingdom. "At this, the administrators and the satraps tried to find grounds for charges against Daniel in his conduct of government affairs, but they were unable to do so"(6:4). Blocked by his integrity, they devised a plan in which that very honesty would be Daniel's undoing. They would use his religion against him.

So they convinced the typically egocentric king to declare a month of monarch worship. During those hallowed days it would be illegal to worship any god or man except Darius. The God-fearing Daniel was trapped. What should he do? He should pray *and give thanks*.

"Now when Daniel learned that the decree had been published, he went home to his upstairs room where the windows opened toward Jerusalem. Three times a day he got down on his knees and prayed, giving thanks to his God, just as he had done before" (6:10).

Before the struggle was over, Daniel would be tossed into the lions' den and given up for dead. You know the rest of the story. His God delivered him from the mouths of the beasts. In the midst of the crisis, Daniel's strategy was simplicity itself. He prayed with thanksgiving. He held on by a "thin thread of thanks."

The thankful prayers were honored.

This teaching is not peculiarly Christian, as you can tell from my reaching back into the Old Testament to recall the example of Daniel. It isn't even peculiarly biblical. Robert Fulghum in his *All I Really Need to Know I Learned in Kindergarten* tells the story of V. P. Menon, who reached the pinnacle of civil service in the days of Britain's rule in India. Menon's story is an illustration of the universality of thanksgiving's efficacy, its ability to transform situations and persons.

A self-made man, Menon rose from his start as a thirteen-year-old laborer through a host of jobs—coal miner, factory hand, merchant, schoolteacher—into Indian government administration. In the process he built a reputation for brilliance and integrity; he was known especially for two characteristics, his impersonal efficiency, and his personal charity.

His daughter explained how his reputation for charity came about. When Menon arrived in Delhi as a young man seeking a position in government, all his possessions, including his money and ID, were stolen at the railroad station. He was faced with the prospect of returning home on foot, defeated. He turned in desperation to an elderly Sikh, soliciting a loan of fifteen rupees to tide him over until he could get a job. The Sikh sympathized with him in his plight. When Menon asked for his address so that he could repay the loan, the Sikh demurred. He told him instead to pay the debt to any stranger who came to him in need, as long as he lived. The help came from a stranger and was to be repaid to a stranger.

Menon never forgot that debt. The day before he died, a beggar came to the family home in Bangalore, asking for help to buy new sandals, for his feet were covered with sores. Menon asked his daughter to take fifteen rupees out of his wallet to give to the man. It was Menon's last conscious act.

Robert Fulghum said he heard the story from a stranger standing beside him in the Bombay airport. Fulghum had come to reclaim his bags at the left-baggage counter, but he had no Indian currency with him, and the agent would not accept a traveler's check. His plane was slated to depart momentarily. Fulghum didn't think he could buy more Indian currency, reclaim his luggage, and still catch his departing plane. The stranger came to his rescue, paid his claim-check fee—about eighty cents—and told Menon's story as he refused any attempt Fulghum made to figure out a way to repay him. The stranger's father had been Menon's assistant and had passed Menon's charitable ways on to his son. The charity traveled "from a nameless Sikh to an Indian civil servant to his assistant to his son to me, a white foreigner in a moment of frustrating inconvenience."[2]

What an incredible breakthrough this hostile world would experience if Menon's exceptional principle would become the rule of human intercourse.

What changes do you suppose were in store for the leper who said thanks for Jesus' healing? What about the other nine? They, too, had been healed—but would they ever experience complete wholeness if they didn't find their way to gratitude?

Have you ever wondered about Lazarus, whom Jesus raised from the dead? How did he express his appreciation?

This much I can tell you about Lawson, who has had so much to learn about giving thanks after losing his son. He will never take things for granted again—not family, not friends, not his job, not the clouds in the sky, nor the beautiful hues and shadows of the distant hills, not the air that he breathes, nor the laughter of a little child. Everything is a reason for giving thanks.

One of the best, and most famous, examples of gratitude, has been frequently told, but the story bears repeating. When Herbert Hoover was a student at Stanford University, the enterprising young entrepreneur ran his own business, a combination lecture and concert forum. On one occasion he contracted for a concert in San Jose with the celebrated and high-priced Polish pianist, Ignace Paderewski. Booking the concert was risky, because Hoover was forced to charge higher than normal admission prices to cover the higher than normal two-thousand-dollar minimum the pianist charged. Hoover expected Paderewski's fame to attract a large enough crowd to cover his costs. But the noted musician didn't draw in California. The crowd was small and so was the gate. Hoover had to come up with four hundred dollars beyond what he took in and what he could personally contribute to meet Paderewski's price. He offered the pianist his personal note to make up the difference; his only collateral was good faith. The great man graciously canceled the obligation and everything ended happily, except that Hoover was penniless for a while.

After being graduated from Stanford, Herbert Hoover went on to a brilliant career in mining and civic service, including wartime work overseeing the feeding of Europe's desperate masses following World War I's devastation. Twenty-five years after the concert in San Jose, a great public reception in Hoover's honor was held in the city of Lodz. By now Paderewski was prime minister of Poland, and in that capacity he thanked the American engineer for having saved tens of thousands of Polish lives. In his response to the President's praise, Mr. Hoover recalled the concert and Mr. Paderewski's generous treatment of him as a young student. The audience applauded loudly. They understood that Hoover's debt to Paderewski had now been paid in full.[3]

This is the question of every grateful heart, isn't it? How do I repay the kindness? V. G. Menon learned that you can't pay it back. You pay it on.

Herbert Hoover couldn't repay his benefactor. He fed his benefactor's people instead.

The woman who survived a nearly fatal accident lives her days in the worship of the God who saved her.

The parents who buried their children have sought for ways to serve others in the name of their children.

Daniel proved that when you can't do anything else in your situation, you can "hang on with a thin thread of thanks."

A grateful heart makes the whole person well.

"And whatever you do, whether in word or deed, do it all in the name of the Lord Jesus, giving thanks to god the Father through him" (Colossians 3:17).

First there is the thanksgiving. Then the victory.

"But thanks be to God! He gives us the victory through our Lord Jesus Christ" (1 Corinthians 15:57).

Chapter 5

When the Coach
Needs Coaching

Acts 18:1-4, 24-28

His throne is the pulpit; he stands in Christ's stead; his message is the word of God; around him are immortal souls; the Savior, unseen is beside him; the Holy Spirit broods over the congregation; angels gaze upon the scene, and heaven and hell await the issue.[1]

Matthew Simpson's description of the awesome, lonely position of the preacher reminds us of the old charge against the minister, that he stands six feet above contradiction. If in fact he is Christ's vicar and his words are the Word of God, who can approach him? Who is his peer? Certainly not the members of the congregation who sit mutely, hearing but never contesting the great man's words. 'Tis not for them to reason why, 'tis but for them to sit and sigh, poor serfs catching a few crumbs from the regal orator's table.

This royal view of preaching is admirable, on the one hand. It underscores the eternal worth of the Word of God. It reminds every Christian that the preaching of the gospel is not to be taken lightly and that the preacher of the gospel is to be respected. On the other hand, if taken too seriously, this veneration of the pulpiteer can become worship of the messenger and not the One from whom the message comes. In its extreme form it leads to the abuses that disgraced the church in the Middle Ages, when the upper clergy were aristocrats and the pope reigned as emperor, his word never to be questioned, his orders never to be disobeyed.

Vestiges of this abuse abound today, even in Protestant, evangelical, independent churches. When churches speak of their pastor as *the* man of God for their church, they enthrone him in a majesty unsupported by scriptural precedent. In the body of Christ as envisioned by the apostle Paul, only Christ receives such homage; all other members of the body are mutually supportive and equally important.

Why this discussion of the role of the minister in a book on victory in Jesus? Because the author is a pastor and has thought long about this subject, and because he believes that what is true in his vocation is true in all fields of endeavor: you never rise above contradiction; you never outgrow the need for a coach. Call that person your mentor, supervisor, critic, teacher, editor, or "pro"; if you desire to keep on growing in insight and ability, you will remain open to a word of correction. The best word comes from God's Word.

Apollos of Alexandria often comes to mind when I'm thinking about the ministry. If ever there was a gifted preacher, it was Apollos. His name even sounds regal—no, more than regal, divine, as in the Greeks' Apollo. This church leader had qualified himself for preaching. "He was a learned man, with a thorough knowledge of the Scriptures. He had been instructed in the way of the Lord, and he spoke with great fervor and taught about Jesus accurately" (Acts 18:24). Learned, deep in Scriptures, knowledgeable about the Lord, a speaker of force and enthusiasm, accurate in his teaching about Jesus. Apollos had it all. Truly, a man of God.

But two of his fellow believers, Priscilla and Aquila, were not awed by his calling, his learning, nor his delivery. They detected a problem: "He knew only the baptism of John." What exactly this means we aren't certain. William Barclay's guess is as good as anyone's.

> He knew of the task Jesus gave men to do but he did not yet fully know of the help Jesus gave men to do it [Barclay is speaking of the Holy Spirit]. He knew of that great call to break with the past; but he did not yet know of that great power to live in the days to come.[2]

Humble tentmakers, Aquila and Priscilla had been with
Paul in Corinth (Acts 18:1-4) and then moved with him to
Ephesus. While with Paul, another learned man, they had
absorbed his teachings about Jesus and believed his teaching
more accurately to reflect the Lord's revelation than Apollos'.
Tactfully they invited Apollos to their home where they could
explain to him "the way of God more adequately." He probably had learned of Jesus through John the Baptist's disciples,
since John's was the only baptism Apollos knew. He seems
to have been ignorant of Peter's Pentecost sermon, or the
Christian practice of being baptized "in the name of Jesus
Christ for the forgiveness of your sins," or Peter's promise
that in doing so "you will receive the gift of the Holy Spirit"
(Acts 2:38).

Apparently Apollos deserves all the good things said of
him in Acts 18, because, as Luke tells the story, the preacher
registers no protest, does not seem to resent his advisors,
but continues to earn the commendation of the saints in
Ephesus to the extent that they can send him on to Achaia
with a letter of recommendation.

His example is good for any minister—or leader in any
field. It is always possible for even the most widely read,
most accomplished, most reputable person to be mistaken.
Teachers also need to be taught. (This author, who makes
his living with his speaking, appreciates both the honesty
and the gentleness of Priscilla and Aquila. They didn't make
a scene, but waited until they could have Apollos in their
home to discuss their points of difference. Considerate
people. In so doing they save Apollos a great deal of future
embarrassment. He will not go on repeating his error.)

Some good counsel comes from this brief episode in the
life of the early church:

Beware of thinking
what everybody else is thinking

Groupthink is not a recent invention. Going along with
the crowd has always been easier than thinking for yourself.
Letting the speaker, who seems to be pleasing everyone else
in the audience by what he is saying, believe he has persuaded

you too is infinitely easier than confronting him with an opposing view.

Thinking what everybody else is thinking is the root of conformity. It afflicts whole cultures. What nation for example, has ever voluntarily admitted it was wrong? A culture is defined by those unchallenged assumptions which govern its thinking. C. S. Lewis, arguing that contemporary readers should read old books so they can get a truer perspective on modern culture, notes that "every age has its own outlook." The old books act as coaches for modern thinkers.

> It is specially good at seeing certain truths and specially liable to make certain mistakes. We all, therefore, need the books that will correct the characteristic mistakes of our own period. And that means the old books. . . . Nothing strikes me more when I read the controversies of past ages than the fact that both sides were usually assuming without question a good deal which we should now absolutely deny. . . . We may be sure that the characteristic blindness of the twentieth century—the blindness about which posterity will ask, 'But how *could* they have thought of that?'—lies where we never suspected it. . . . None of us can fully escape this blindness, but we shall certainly increase it, and weaken our guard against it, if we read only modern books.[3]

Lewis's warning reminds us of some of the assumptions that the majority of Americans have blindly accepted in the course of the last fifty years. I still shudder when I recall an anti-communism speech I delivered with much fervency and conviction in the late 1950s. I had swallowed completely the propaganda of the McCarthy era, much to my later embarrassment. Think of how America's views have changed regarding racial equality, the role of women, the nature of the family, the omnipotence of communism, acceptable sexual behavior, and the virtue of unregulated capitalism. Yet there was a time when presuppositions concerning each of these were practically unchallenged. Change was brought about because in time a few outspoken persons quit thinking what everyone else was thinking.

Some of today's "givens" will be transformed one day in the same way, and our descendants will indeed marvel, "How *could* they have thought that?"

Beware of thinking you've already thought it all

Apollos earns our admiration because of his apparent openness to new information from Aquila and Priscilla. He did not make the mistake of so many experts: he did not assume he had already thought of everything.

The humility of the great historian Will Durant is instructive. "Sixty years ago," he said, "I knew everything; now I know nothing; education is a progressive discovery of our own ignorance."[4] Anyone who has waded through Durant's tomes is duly impressed with his great learning; anyone familiar with his life is impressed that into the tenth decade of his life the indefatigable scholar was still searching out new information, never satisfied with the state of his learning.

In matters of faith, however, it is astonishing how many people are content to rest on the smattering of biblical information they picked up as Sunday school children. They know all they want to know; furthermore, if a preacher or anyone else offers a different perspective on what they already know or offers new information that challenges their present state of knowledge, they resist or reject the challenge to their complacency with amazing stubbornness. They will not be moved.

Dostoyevsky picks up this theme in his novel, *The Idiot*. "You know," said Prince Myshkin, (whom Dostoyevsky develops as a Christ-figure),

> in my opinion, it's sometimes quite a good thing to be absurd. Indeed, it's much better; it makes it so much easier to forgive each other and to humble ourselves. One can't start straight with perfection! To attain perfection, one must first of all be able not to understand many things. *For if we understand things too quickly, we may perhaps fail to understand them well enough.*[5]

At first we have a little trouble understanding the prince's point, just as the characters in the story do. After reflecting, though, we appreciate his wisdom. Our problem is not so much in understanding things too quickly as in *thinking* we do.

Another Russian, Yakov Smirnoff in his book, *America on Six Rubles a Day*, humorously makes Dostoyevsky's same point. In visiting our country, Smirnoff said, he was not prepared for "the incredible variety of products available in American grocery stores." On Smirnoff's first shopping trip he saw powdered milk, something quite new to him. You just add water and you get milk. Then he saw powdered orange juice. You just add water and you get orange juice. Then he saw baby powder, and thought to himself, "What a country!"[6]

He understood too quickly, so he didn't understand at all!

The Old Testament prophet Hosea bewailed his nation's ignorance: the people "are destroyed from lack of knowledge."

> Because you have rejected knowledge,
> I also reject you as my priests;
> because you have ignored the law of your God,
> I also will ignore your children (Hosea 4:6).

Had you asked Hosea's countrymen, they would have protested their innocence. Of course they had knowledge of God. Certainly they were not ignorant of His laws. They were, after all, descendants of Abraham and Moses.

They thought they had already thought it all. Perhaps they knew but had just forgotten Proverbs 18:15: "The heart of the discerning acquires knowledge; the ears of the wise seek it out."

Beware of thinking your credentials have qualified you

Apparently Apollos did not stand on ceremony. He was the learned scholar from Alexandria, the world's cultural center in his day. He knew Jewish Scriptures and Greek culture. Who were Aquila and Priscilla, anyway, but unlettered tentmakers? They worked with their hands; he was an intellectual.

Apollos's apparent humility is an admirable characteristic, especially to this writer who has spent no little time among intellectuals. Not all bookish types would agree that only the educated have a right to speak, but enough of them give that impression to earn all academe an unsavory reputation.

Many of them, however, would agree with the philosopher
Bertrand Russell, "Men are born ignorant, not stupid; they
are made stupid by their education."[7] Too strong a statement,
undoubtedly, but not untruthful, either, especially when we
allow our amassing of credits and degrees to displace a more
worthy search for God's truth. Evidently God has never been
unduly impressed with mere intelligence, nor has He limited
himself to working through people with proper credentials.
Jesus was on to His Father's method, "I praise you, Father,
Lord of heaven and earth, because you have hidden these
things from the wise and learned, and revealed them to little
children. Yes, Father, for this was your good pleasure" (Luke
10:21).

So we ministers are well advised to listen to our untutored
parishioners, and veteran politicians are wise to consult the
grass roots, and physicians dare not turn a deaf ear to their
patients.

I like Albert Einstein stories. Widely acclaimed to possess
one of the keenest minds in the twentieth century, the great
physicist was nonetheless a humble student to the end of his
days. He was never satisfied that he knew enough and never
too proud to learn from others. One time the Russian physicist Joffe traveled to Berlin to visit Einstein. Joffe had come
to describe his recent work on the mechanical and electrical
properties of crystals. Einstein was fascinated. When the
Russian arrived at his house at about three o'clock in the
afternoon, the older scientist asked him to explain his work
in detail. Joffe did so for the next two hours. When Mrs.
Einstein broke into Joffe's presentation to tell her husband
that visitors from Hamburg would be coming to see Einstein
around five o'clock, he led Joffe to a nearby park where they
could continue uninterrupted; they returned only after they
were certain the visitors were gone.

Joffe talked for two straight hours longer. Then the discussion began. They ate their evening meal at eight o'clock,
but even during the meal (with his wife instructing the pre-
occupied Einstein where to stick his fork, how to eat his
macaroni) the talking did not stop. The discussion continued
to midnight—and past. Finally at two in the morning, after

Joffe had missed his train, the discussion ended. Einstein had been able to assimilate the new information into his understanding of how the universe works.[8]

This took place years after Einstein had published his famous relativity theory, and years after his fame had become worldwide. Yet he was still restlessly seeking new information, unimpressed with his own credentials. He wanted to know the truth.

Jesus castigated the religious leaders of His day for doing exactly the opposite. Claiming to have the final word on the things of God, they stifled learning, at least learning that was not under their control. Jesus was on to them, too.

"Woe to you experts in the law, because you have taken away the key to knowledge. You yourselves have not entered, and you have hindered those who were entering" (Luke 11:52).

Credentials can too easily become a substitute for, rather than a mark of, expertise.

Beware of thinking
your thinking is infallible

John Warwick Montgomery's tragi-comic parable of willful ignorance says it all. There was once a man who thought he was dead. His obsession deeply concerned his wife and friends, who packed him off to a psychiatrist. The counselor was persuaded he could cure his deluded patient. His strategy was to convince him of one simple fact, one that flatly contradicted his notion that he was dead. Dead men, he repeatedly assured his patient, do not bleed. He prescribed a regimen for his patient. He was to read medical tests, observe autopsies, and so on, until he could see for himself that dead men do not bleed. At the end of weeks of this straightforward treatment, the patient finally admitted, "All right, all right! You've convinced me. Dead men do not bleed."

He was ready. The psychiatrist stuck him in the arm with a needle, and the blood flowed. Stricken, the man observed the red stream coursing down his forearm and cried out with an ashen face, "Good Lord! Dead men bleed after all!"[9]

Montgomery's story recalls the foolish advice the shallow

Polonius gives his son Laertes in Shakespeare's *Hamlet*—
advice, by the way, often quoted in our foolish age as wisdom:
"To thine own self be true." The "dead" man was doing just
that, and his stubborn insistence on his own lifelessness
made it impossible for reality to penetrate his consciousness.
"I gotta be me" and "I gotta do my own thing" are the pitiful
bleatings of the misdirected. If nothing else, they betray full
confidence in one's own thinking, confidence without foundation.

If you are ever tempted to pit your personal thinking
against everyone else's—like the living dead man—or even
more dangerously, against God's, check out a few Scriptures
to learn what God thinks of the proud. Here are some good
reminders:

> He guides the humble in what is right
>   and teaches them his way.   Psalm 25:9

> The wise in heart accept commands,
>   but a chattering fool comes to ruin.   Proverbs 10:8

> When pride comes, then comes disgrace,
>   but with humility comes wisdom.   Proverbs 11:2

> The way of a fool seems right to him,
>   but a wise man listens to advice.   Proverbs 12:15

> Before his downfall a man's heart is proud,
>   but humility comes before honor.   Proverbs 18:12

> Do not be quick with your mouth,
>   do not be hasty in your heart to utter
>   anything before God.
> God is in heaven
>   and you are on earth,
>   so let your words be few.   Ecclesiastes 5:2

For whoever exalts himself will be humbled, and whoever
humbles himself will be exalted.   Matthew 23:12

Do not deceive yourselves. If any one of you thinks he is
wise by the standards of this age, he should become a "fool"
so that he may become wise.   1 Corinthians 3:18

Who is wise and understanding among you? Let him show
it by his good life, by deeds done in the humility that comes
from wisdom. But if you harbor bitter envy and selfish ambition in your hearts, do not boast about it or deny the truth.
Such "wisdom" does not come down from heaven but is
earthly, unspiritual, of the devil. For where you have envy and
selfish ambition, there you find disorder and every evil practice.   James 3:13-16

Young men, in the same way be submissive to those who
are older. All of you, clothe yourselves with humility toward
one another, because,
    "God opposes the proud
        but gives grace to the humble."
Humble yourselves, therefore, under God's mighty hand,
that he may lift you up in due time.   1 Peter 5:5, 6

Add these verses together, and they (and many, many more
that could have been selected) are a convincing argument
that the secret of personal strength is not found in seeking to
promote or to please oneself, but rather we must:

Seek to please the worthiest

President George Washington, universally admired even in
his own age (a rare accomplishment for a holder of high public office), named as his favorite play Joseph Addison's *Cato*.
In it there's a character named Juba, a Numidian (and therefore not a Roman, which is the critical point) who seeks the
approval of the Roman Cato because, as he says, he would
rather have the approval of that one man than riches or anything else. He has learned that far better than being true to
oneself is being true to others, and most particularly to the
wise and just.
    Would such a play be tolerated in today's poll-infested
political environment?

In a different field, book reviewing, Clifton Fadiman says something similar. Challenging Francis Bacon's bromide, "reading maketh a full man," Fadiman protests that the truth is exactly the opposite. Any reviewer like himself "who has been in harness for twenty years or so" will assure you "Bacon was just dreaming up sentences." Fadiman estimates he has read five or ten thousand books—"it doesn't matter which" over twenty years. There's no merit in it, he admits. "Every so often I catch myself wondering whether I shouldn't be a sight wiser if I had read only fifteen, and they the right ones."[10]

Centuries earlier the Greek philosopher Epictetus scolded a young man who was giving himself airs in the theater. "I am wise," he bragged, "for I have conversed with many wise men."

Epictetus rejoined, "I too have conversed with many rich men, yet I am not rich!"

A few pages back I was arguing that we need to be open to new information from others who can teach us. I ridiculed the man so convinced he was dead that he couldn't be persuaded otherwise. Now, though, I sound as if I'm arguing just the contrary: you can listen to too many advisers, read too many books. No contradiction. Thomas Nixon Carver used to teach agricultural economics at Harvard. He proposed what he called Carver's Law: "The trouble with radicals is that they only read radical literature, and the trouble with conservatives is that they don't read anything."[11]

Now you see the issue. Too much of the wrong (or biased, or partisan) reading is not good for you, and no reading may be even worse. Whose words are worthy, then, of our attention?

The psalmist's prayer is the right one:

> Send forth *your* light and *your* truth,
> let them guide me;
> let them bring me to *your* holy mountain,
> to the place where *you* dwell.   Psalm 43:3

Teach me *your* way, O Lord,
   and I will walk in *your* truth;
give me an undivided heart,
   that I may fear *your* name.   Psalm 86:11

Here is the solution: the light, the truth, the holiness, the way to be discovered in God's Word. He's "the worthiest." Seek to please Him, to think His thoughts after Him, to do His will on earth. Join the saints in eternity who, having found the truth, stick with Him.

"You are worthy, our Lord and God,
   to receive glory and honor and power,
for you created all things,
   and by your will they were created
   and have their being."   Revelation 4:11

Chapter 6

How Can I Know
What God Wants?

Acts 8:26-39

To seek victory in Jesus is to seek God's will. A victorious life can't be achieved by a Christian who either willingly or unwittingly opposes God's purposes. Therefore it's imperative that we spend a little time exploring how we can know what His will is.

We approach the subject cautiously, because it has been so badly misunderstood. I'm equally wary around persons who protest complete confidence in their ability to discern God's will in everything (I for one can't claim to have such ability) and other persons who are forever asking, "How can anyone *know* God's will?" I can't help wondering whether they really want to know. Would they do it if they found it?

Perhaps they would. Then again, maybe they wouldn't. Their question could mean one of the following:

1. They really are searching with all their hearts to know what He would have them do.

2. They are mildly curious, hoping to discover a grand scheme for their lives that they will pursue if the rewards are great enough to compensate for any costs involved.

3. They are anxious, fearing God is going to make some

extraordinary demand they have neither desire nor ability to satisfy.

4. They have no intention of changing anything, but they like to sound like believers while maintaining full control.

5. They don't believe it's possible to know the will of God, so they raise the question in order to explain it away. Thus they justify continuing in their current lifestyles.

6. They believe they are doing everything they know to be obedient disciples of Jesus, but they are facing a crisis in their personal relationships or their occupations or finances and are seeking satisfaction for their particular needs of the moment.

If it's specific answers they are after, they're doomed to disappointment. Solutions seldom arrive as if by divine fiat. More often than not, understanding of God's participation in an event comes only later. This apparent delay leads some petitioners to doubt God interests himself in personal affairs, even though Scriptures teach that our concerns are His.

While we agonize over questions of God's will, He has already provided many answers in His Word. The Bible clearly labels some things "the will of God":

✔ We know He wants us to love Him and to love our neighbors as ourselves (Matthew 22:34-40).

✔ We know that when we do God's will we become members of the family of God, brothers and sisters of Christ (Mark 3:35).

✔ We know we are not to conform "to the pattern of this world, but be transformed by the renewing" of our minds, thus testing and approving "what God's will is—his good, pleasing and perfect will" (Romans 12:2).

✔ We know that we are to give ourselves "first to the Lord and then [to others] in keeping with God's will" (2 Corinthians 8:5).

✔ We know "it is God's will that you should be sanctified: that you should avoid sexual immorality; that each of you should learn to control his own body in a way that is holy and honorable, not in passionate lust like the heathen, who do not know God" (1 Thessalonians 4:3-5).

✔ We know we are to "be joyful always; pray continually; [and] give thanks in all circumstances, for this is God's will for you in Christ Jesus" (1 Thessalonians 5:16-18).

✔ We know we are to "silence the ignorant talk of foolish men" by doing good (1 Peter 2:15).

✔ We know it is better "to suffer for doing good than for doing evil" (1 Peter 3:17).

✔ We know that we can be assured of His love and His desire that none should be lost (Matthew 25).

All these things and more, we know.

The book of Acts contains the accounts of many conversions. Men and women from divergent backgrounds learn of God's will for their lives—and give themselves to it. Luke includes their stories in his chronicles of the growth of the early church, along with statistical evidence of the explosive growth (first three thousand members, then four thousand and so on). His concern is not statistical; rather, he is a believer and a physician who is keenly interested in individuals, especially in their transformation when touched by the Spirit of God.

The conversion of an Ethiopian official is one of Luke's most interesting accounts. From beginning to end of this brief story, the court official is bold in seeking to know God's will and in readiness to obey Him. As soon as he understands, he obeys.

He openly declares himself for God

The official is either a God-fearer or a proselyte. As a God-fearer, he may be one of a large number of persons attracted by the Jewish religion's teaching that there is only one God, or he may even have gone the next step and become a proselyte, one who has submitted to circumcision and allowed himself to be known as a convert to Judaism. He is returning from Jerusalem, where he worshiped in the temple.

Not that there is any shortage of religions back home in Ethiopia. He seeks something his homeland can't offer, however. The Jewish teaching that "the Lord, he is one God" with its high ethical tone appeals to him as the polytheistic gods of his homeland do not. (The Ethiopia of the New Testament is called Cush in the Old. It's a land lying along the upper Nile, known more recently as Nubia. It's not exactly contiguous with today's Ethiopia). He wants to know and worship the true God and, as his journey to Jerusalem testifies, he is not secretive about his religious yearning.

He commits himself, at some personal expense

His declaration for God is not mere lip service. To travel from the upper Nile was no casual undertaking in his day. He "puts his money where his mouth is," laying out the financial and physical price to make his strenuous journey to the holy city. He's not at all like certain Sunday-go-to-meeting Christians some poet has satirized:

They do it every Sunday,
They'll be all right on Monday;
It's just a little habit they've acquired.

Not for him the "cheap grace" of believers who want the blessings God offers without making the sacrifices He expects. Not for him, either, the praising of other people's sacrifices in lieu of his own. He has chosen to worship the rather austere God of the Jews, with His high moral expectations, even though much easier routes to the gods lie all around him back home.

William Barclay recounts the unusual conversion story of G. ffrench Beytagh, the former Dean of Johannesburg who later gained notoriety in his South African homeland for his fearless stands against *apartheid*. He had once lived an erratic life, which explains what he was doing in a bar at midnight, when this pivotal event took place. It was his turn to treat, but his drinking companion refused Beytagh's offer of another drink because, he said after consulting his watch, "It is after midnight and I am going to make my Communion in church this morning."

Barclay says that Beytagh "was shattered." Even though his partner was drinking, he stopped in order to fast until early Communion. More than that, in a hotel bar he was not afraid to say so. "This man's religion affected his life."[1] You and I might have wished it had affected him enough to keep him out of the bar, but Beytagh had not been accustomed to seeing a man governed in any way by his religion, and he was so moved that Barclay refers to this episode as "the experience which brought him [Beytagh] to the Church."

The Ethiopian official's religious commitment seems to have been made of similar material.

He doesn't limit
his commitment to public worship

Luke tells us he has already been to worship. He has done his duty. He is not satisfied with the minimum, though. He thirsts to know more of God, as his Bible reading on the road home from Jerusalem signifies. He has studied with other sincere believers in Judaism's holy city, but his yearning for more is unsatisfied. In this respect he represents countless seekers after righteousness who can't get enough of the Bible. They are in as many worship services as their church offers each week, and then they seek out others. They join small Bible study groups, they listen to Christian radio stations and watch Christian TV programs. Then, their craving unfilled, they take their Bibles to work with them and sit during their coffee and lunch breaks at a table in the lunchroom and study by themselves. You just can't get too much of a good thing, they explain. They have found in the Bible something extraordinary, truly exciting, and they want more.

Their reverence for the written Word of the Lord is akin to awe. A singular moment in the life of Alexander Tvardovsky, editor-in-chief of the Russian literary magazine *Novy Mir,* made me think of the many dedicated Bible students I have known. One evening in 1962 he took home a pile of manuscripts to read in bed. He thumbed through them quickly, as editors are wont to do, scanning the first few pages, making snap judgments and tossing them on a mounting pile of rejects. Then he came to one he couldn't toss. The author was unknown to him, and the title was deceptively simple: *One Day in the Life of Ivan Denisovich.* Here was something extraordinary. He read ten lines and had to stop. Later he told a friend, "Suddenly I felt that I couldn't read it like this. I had to do something appropriate to the occasion. So I got up. I put on my best black suit, a white shirt with a starched collar, a tie and my good shoes. Then I sat at my desk and read a new classic."[2]

Today Aleksandr Solzhenitsyn is regarded by most Western readers as Russia's greatest contemporary author. The literary critic saw in Solzhenitsyn's novel something of greatness. He responded appropriately.

The government official from Ethiopia saw something in the Bible that piqued his curiosity, commanded his respect, and created a craving to understand more. He responded appropriately.

Although a high government official, he accepts guidance in spiritual matters

As we have noted in earlier chapters, it is difficult for those who have achieved a certain rank of prestige or power to humble themselves enough to accept spiritual guidance from others, especially from others who aren't their peers. This official was no mean functionary. His American equivalent today would be the Secretary of the Treasury; in Britain his title would be Chancellor of the Exchequer. The governing myth of Egyptian politics held the Pharaoh to be too sacred (he was considered the child of the sun) to do secular things himself. Thus Candace, the queen mother, acted on her son's behalf as virtual ruler of the government. This official works directly for her.

We aren't certain whether he is a literal eunuch (a castrated man) or is called one simply by virtue of his office (the queen's assistants were usually eunuchs). He probably is one, but the question is irrelevant. His high office is not; it makes his openness to Philip's teaching all the more impressive.

He has opened his scroll at Isaiah 53, a favorite of today's Christians, who view it as one of the great messianic prophecies of the Old Testament. Philip uses this passage concerning the coming Suffering Servant to speak to the official about Jesus.

The national leader becomes Philip's humble student. His willingness to learn is admirable.

Willingness to learn constitutes the difference between success and failure in many areas of life. Let me tell you about how Ron Mehl became willing. I would like to tell you that Ron Mehl is my friend, because the dynamic Beaverton, Oregon, minister impressed me so much on the one occasion we spent some time together. That claim would be stretching the truth. The best I can say is that some of our very best friends attend his church, and our friend Bill (an incurable golf addict) and Ron play the same course. It's one of Ron's golfing stories that comes to mind as I think of the Ethiopian official's teachableness.

As an devoted non-golfer myself, I have to take Ron's word for it that the Cypress Point Golf Course on the Monterey Peninsula is "one of the most scenic and beautifully-groomed courses on the planet." He describes the "stunning seascapes [that] loom at every turn, the deer running wild, the seals playing along the beach and the dolphins and whales spouting and frolicking just offshore." A golfer's paradise, in other words, so when Ron was presented with the opportunity to play there, he jumped at it.

Cypress Point, at least in those days, had an inviolable club rule. A caddie was required. Ron had never used one before and didn't like the idea. He thought himself a duffer and knew that any caddie at this prestigious club would have trailed some of the greatest legends of golf. To make matters worse, the caddie he drew was old enough to be his grandfather. What memories of other golfers' prowess he would have! As I said, Ron didn't like the idea of being compared with any of them.

Unsurprisingly, Ron, a nervous youngster by comparison, got off to a bad start. On the second hole, he discovered his caddie's name (Ed) and age (sixty-eight). When Ron asked Ed how far he thought Ron was from hole, the caddie told him 163 yards. Ron wasn't buying. He knew it "wasn't a foot less than 185 yards." So early in the game, and he was already beginning to doubt this Ed. Ron took out his five-iron and hit it nearly 185 yards—over the green and into a patch of rocks near the beach. Ed quietly replaced his divot.

For the next hole Ed said, "It's 189 yards," barely looking up from the club he was cleaning. Ron knew Ed's eyesight had to be failing for sure. He could tell the hole was not an inch over 170 yards away. So he hit it 170 yards—and watched his ball land at least fifteen yards short. Ed polished his putter.

Now Ron had to read the green. He saw other caddies helping their players read their putts. He didn't want to seem bitter—there wasn't great warmth between player and caddie by now—so he asked Ed which way he thought the ball would roll, right or left of cup? "Left," said Ed, "toward the ocean." Ron thought he was mocking him, because the ground was obviously slanted to the right. Relying on his own judgment, he putted—and missed.

By now Ed had had enough. "Son," he explained, "I think you need to make a decision here, and soon. Because if you don't, it's going to be a long day for both of us. See, I have one job. Every day I walk this course and tell people how far they have to hit the ball. That's it. That's all I do. I don't have to mow, I don't have to fertilize, and I don't have to make sandwiches at the clubhouse. I leave those things to the people who know how to do them, and they leave the guessing of yardage to me.

"I've walked this course for over fifty years and I know every tree and every blade of grass. And when I say 167 yards, I don't mean 169. What you have to do is decide if you are going to trust me or not."

With that, he replaced Ron's putter in the bag and walked on to the next tee.

Ron decided to trust him. His game improved dramatically.[3]

To trust or not to trust a caddie isn't a life-or-death decision, although some of my golfing friends might think so. Where you and I might identify with Ron's experience is in a willingness to trust another's spiritual counsel. At least this is my problem. I've been to Bible college and I've taught in several. I've read the great authorities in biblical scholarship and I've done some writing of my own. And then in some study group some high school graduate holds forth with an interpretation of a passage of Scripture that directly contradicts what I know to be the real meaning of the verses. It's not easy to remain open-minded in such moments.

How easy can it have been for a high government official to sit meekly at Deacon Philip's feet?

A recent political prophet on the world scene is Václav Havel, the Czech playwright who became president of his country in the collapse of the USSR. I don't know whether Havel has been a successful leader or not, but I have been impressed enough with his thoughtfulness to read him whenever he appears in print in English. He offered a little insight into his philosophy and character in one essay in which he quotes Patocka (who is unknown to me), who once told him, "The real test of a man is not how well he plays the role he has invented for himself, but how well he plays the role that destiny assigned to him."[4]

The self-made man or woman earns our praise, but in limited doses. To invent yourself, to hack your way through the wilderness of opportunity, to pursue your dreams until they turn to reality, to overcome obstacles and dominate circumstances to become what you want to be, this is worthy of praise. But there is another achiever who deserves more. This is the person who refuses to be confined to the limiting, incomplete, unbalanced role that the ego concocts and then chains us to but instead seeks to play the role God has assigned, to pursue the opportunity His providence presents, even if it doesn't seem in character. The Ethiopian could so easily have disdained to hear Philip: "I'm a high government official. How can one in my position allow himself to become the student of one of no position at all, like yourself?"

He remains humble enough to learn a surprising truth

The most amazing part of the story is that anyone in a power position like the official's would be attracted to following a suffering Son of God:

> Who, being in very nature God,
> did not consider equality with God
> something to be grasped,
> but made himself nothing,
> taking the very nature of a servant,
> being made in human likeness (Philippians 2:6, 7).

"Being in very nature God." God, divinity, majesty, lordship —these words do not fill the mind with images of service, sacrifice, or suffering. What would the Ethiopian think if Philip were to quote Jesus' words on officialdom?

> You know that those who are regarded as rulers of the Gentiles lord it over them, and their high officials exercise authority over them. Not so with you. Instead, whoever wants to become great among you must be your servant, and whoever wants to be first must be slave of all. For even the Son of Man did not come to be served, but to serve, and to give his life as a ransom for many (Mark 10:42-45).

Luke doesn't report very much of Philip's interpretation of the Isaiah passage, but Philip could not do justice to the Scripture without presenting Jesus as a most unusual Messiah. The official, one of the "rulers of the Gentiles," learns that God's anointed one did not come with His legions to govern a dominion of this world. Instead, "he was led like a lamb to the slaughter, and as a sheep before her shearers is silent, so he did not open his mouth" (Isaiah 53:7).

Starting with this remarkable verse, Philip tells the Ethiopian of a remarkable Master who leads those who believe in Him to victorious living. In the hands of Philip, the mysterious book becomes a missal of love.

Mildred Welshimer Phillips, longtime dean of women at Milligan College, was one of my favorite storytellers, so I was pleased when she published a book of her speeches. Daughter of the legendary P. H. Welshimer, longtime minister (over fifty-five years, I think) of the First Christian Church of Canton, Ohio, Mildred knew most of the leading preachers of her father's era as well as her own, and she loved talking about them. One of her stories was first told by a Mr. Knepper, one of her father's contemporaries. He often repeated it in his evangelistic meetings. He said he was visiting in a home in Ohio when he spotted a book on the table. As most preachers would have done, he picked it up and glanced through it. The young woman in the home said her boyfriend had given it to her as a birthday present, but she admitted she didn't care much about it. She'd rather have received a box of candy. As she talked, Mr. Knepper continued to leaf through it. Certain underlined sentences caught his attention. "I love you," said one sentence. So did another. "I long to see you" was underlined in yet another. And so the underlining went through the book.

"Well!" Mr. Knepper said, "Have you noticed these passages that this friend of yours has underscored?" No, she admitted, she had never read the book.

"Do you know what this book is? That young fellow who gave it to you is bashful, so he gave you the book, so by reading it you could see how much he loves you."

"Give me the book!" she said, rather peremptorily.

The evangelist said he last saw her running outside to read it under a tree. It had become a new book.[5]

In a similar fashion Philip helps the official to read Isaiah 53 as a love letter, an Old Testament precursor to John 3:16, "For God so loved the world that he gave his one and only Son." The official has never looked at God this way before.

As soon as he understands what to do, he does it

Luke's narrative is terse. He doesn't tell us what Philip said about conversion to Christ, about the meaning of baptism, or much else. Just the bare essentials. What is clear is that the Ethiopian official is convinced. "Look, here is water. Why shouldn't I be baptized?"

Once persuaded, he has to do something. Baptism affords that opportunity. Baptism is many things. A government official would naturally see it as an act of obeisance to a sovereign. He has come to believe Jesus is Lord. He must demonstrate it. For him, baptism is the means of publicly placing himself under that Sovereign's sway as he had earlier knelt to Candace, the queen mother. He who has such a powerful position in Ethiopia is submitting himself to an even higher authority than the one he serves in Egypt.

Let the Lord be Lord

In this chapter we've been exploring the role of human will in relation to God's will. The official is willingly submitting to the lordship of Jesus through his baptism. God's will, rather than his own, he now seeks to serve. He who has obviously been driven by strong will power (you don't get to be Secretary of the Treasury if you're a wimp), is giving up his *willfulness* in relation to God and proving his *willingness* to let the Lord be Lord.

That does not mean he has somehow become a passive personality. He has rather become a persuaded personality, and is acting on the new conviction. The Greek language yields an insight missing in English. It has three verb voices (active, passive, and middle); English has only two, active and passive. The voices the two languages have in common work the same way:

Active: *I counsel my friend.* I am the subject of the sentence, and I do the acting, hence the *active* voice.

Passive: *I am counseled by* my friend. In this sentence, I am still the subject of the sentence, but I don't do the action. I am acted upon. My friend does the acting. I am the passive recipient of his action, hence the verb is said to be in the passive voice.

What English lacks is the helpful middle voice of the Greek. *I take counsel.* In this sentence, the subject I is both acted upon *(my friend counsels me)* and acts *(I seek and thoughtfully take advice).* Two wills are involved, each respecting the other.

As an administrator of a church and a college, I have many occasions to use the middle voice. I have decisions to make for which I have inadequate information or insight, so I seek the best advice I can get. Then I make the decision.

The counsel I receive is often contradictory, one respected advisor disagreeing with another. I have to choose among the options. I say of all the advice my several colleagues give me, "I have taken counsel." Then of the one whose argument has persuaded me to his or her point of view I will say, "I am taking ___'s counsel on this issue." That's the advice I choose to act on.

In my own case, I'm afraid I'm stubborn enough to insist, "Nobody's gonna tell me what to do!" I don't take direct orders very well. But I can listen and am open to persuasion.

This seems to be the stance of the Ethiopian official. He's a good listener. He takes counsel. Then, persuaded by Philip's teaching, which must incorporate much of what Peter taught on the Day of Pentecost (see Acts 2), he willingly acts on the truth he now believes.

An early Christian tradition reports that the official returned home and evangelized Ethiopia. We don't know for certain. What we do know from the Scripture is that he went on his way rejoicing. If the tradition is accurate, so did Philip.

Chapter 7

Why Does It Take So Long to Get It Right?

Matthew 16:13-23

My childhood question was, "What am I going to be when I grow up?"

My adulthood question is, "What am I going to be when I grow up?"

My wife's question about me, asked in wonderment and dismay the day I came in, scratched and bleeding, from my latest escapade on a three-wheeler (when it rode me upside down into a blackberry-covered ravine), was, "Won't you ever grow up?"

Fair questions. For nearly six decades now I've been trying to become a success, to learn from my failures, to grow in Jesus, to "get it right." I'm not there yet.

Sound familiar? Don't you also sometimes feel as if you're never going to become the kind of person, let alone the kind of Christian, you want to be? We're in good company, you and I. One of America's most famous and most influential preachers was Dwight L. Moody, who lamented, "The man I have more trouble with than anybody else is D. L. Moody." Sometimes he just felt he'd never get it right.

A *New Yorker* cartoon captures the mood. A minister is

explaining the creation of things to his congregation. "Having completed the formation of the earth, on the seventh day the Lord rested. Then, on the eighth day, the Lord said, 'Let there be problems.' *And there were problems.*"[1] The cartoonist was right about the problems, but wrong about their origin. We, not God, bring most of them on ourselves.

One of my favorite examples comes from the early days of Zip Codes, when the U. S. Postal Department, in an effort to promote their use, used Bill Keane's "Little Jeffy" on trucks and billboards. He appeared all over the country in a sleeper suit that was open down the front. "Don't forget to ZIP it," he winsomely reminded postal patrons. But when the postmaster general sent Mr. Keane a letter of gratitude and two souvenir copies of the poster, both mailings had the wrong Zip Code!

Do you ever have such days?

I have them regularly, which is probably why I identify so much with another favorite, the impulsive, terribly human apostle Peter, who stumbles through the pages of the Gospels like a spiritual toddler learning to walk. Obviously a strong natural leader, Peter has a predictable need to be the first with the most. His personality dominates the Gospels with a force second only to that of Jesus. Of all the disciples, it's Peter you remember most vividly.

In this chapter we're going to concentrate on Matthew 16:13-23. But before we do, consider Peter's dramatic role in the second half of this Gospel.

In chapter 14, he walks on water, briefly.

In chapter 17, along with James and John, he stares at the incredible sight of a transfigured Jesus. Only Peter speaks. He proposes they construct some shrines to capture the moment for history.

In chapter 26 Peter is all over the place:

He boasts he'll never disown Jesus, no matter what. Jesus is not persuaded (31-35).

Peter falls asleep in Gethsemane, in spite of his best intentions (36-46).

He disowns Jesus, just as his Lord has predicted (69-75).

What are we to conclude about this eager, bumbling student? Here he is in the last days of Jesus' ministry, and he still does not seem to be getting it right.

Let's return to Matthew 16, which contains one of the New Testament's most critical passages, the scene of the Good Confession. Here's Peter, again, this time uttering words that will guide church history for millennia to come: "You are the Christ, the Son of the living God." We often hear these words repeated as someone is baptized into Christ. By this juncture in their ministry together, Peter, who has seen Jesus heal the sick, teach the masses, and raise the dead, has become convinced Jesus is indeed the promised Messiah whose coming the prophets foretold.

"Blessed are you, Simon son of Jonah," Jesus commends him. He affirms the truth of Peter's confession. The disciple hasn't come to this conclusion on his own, Jesus tells him. God gave him the words. So important are Peter's words of confession, Jesus says that the future of His work on earth will rest on them.

How proud Peter must feel. He has spoken eternal truth and Jesus has publicly congratulated him.

Too proud, it seems. Just a few sentences later that same Master sternly reprimands him. "Get behind me, Satan!"

To a casual reader it must seem almost as if Jesus is suffering mood swings. Peter intends no harm. To the contrary, he's trying to protect his teacher. Jesus was preparing His friends for His eventual suffering and death in Jerusalem. "Never, Lord!" Peter protests. "This shall never happen to you!"

As I said, Peter means well. Convinced that Jesus is the Messiah, his protest is a form of commitment to him. "Not to worry, Lord. We'll protect You. God'll protect You. You have a mission to fulfill, a great work to accomplish. You won't be allowed—we won't allow You—to die in Jerusalem."

But Jesus and Peter don't have the same conception of the messianic method. To Peter, the Christ can't be other than all-powerful. He has seen the power, he knows what Jesus can do. Surely His enemies in Jerusalem will be helpless against Him.

For Jesus, the Messiah has not come so much to display His strength as to suffer in order to save. Peter's is a very human point of view. Do things, shake things, move things. Jesus' is the more surprising, more permanent point of view: love people, serve God, suffer much, and trust the heavenly Father to guarantee the outcome.

"Get behind me, Satan!" Jesus is not talking to Peter. He's talking through him, to the satanic influence on him. His words carry us back to the Judean wilderness and His agonizing forty days there where again and again Jesus had to fight back Satan's subtle enticements. Always the human way is easier, more glamorous than God's way.

What a contrast between Peter, who had such a hard time getting it right, and Jesus, who had it right all the time. What's the Lord to do with such a slow learner?

He makes a winner of him, that's what He does.

The angel at Jesus' empty tomb singles out Peter for special attention: "Go, tell his disciples and Peter, 'He is going ahead of you into Galilee'" (Mark 16:7). One of the resurrected Lord's first priorities is to make certain Peter knows that his denial will not forever bar him from his Master's company.

Jesus reinstates Peter in the quietly moving reconciliation scene in John 21:15-20. "Feed my sheep," He tells him. "You are still my disciple. I am counting on you to carry on in my absence. You made a mistake, but that was yesterday and now we are together again—and forever. Feed my sheep."

When Dr. Luke commences his history of the early church in the book of Acts, he presents Peter in his role as the dynamic leader of the apostles. Acts 2 records the opening of the church doors with Peter's sermon on the Day of Pentecost. Peter has finally got it right.

I often review this man's incredible career when I am discouraged with my own. "If there was hope for Peter, there's hope for me," is my reasoning. I turn to the apostle Paul's confessional in Romans 7:14-25, for the same reason:

> We know that the law is spiritual; but I am unspiritual, sold as a slave to sin. I do not understand what I do. For what I want to do I do not do, but what I hate I do. And if I do what I do not want to do, I agree that the law is good. As it is, it is no longer I myself who do

it, but it is sin living in me. I know that nothing good lives in me, that is, in my sinful nature. For I have the desire to do what is good, but I cannot carry it out. For what I do is not the good I want to do; no, the evil I do not want to do—this I keep on doing. Now if I do what I do not want to do, it is no longer I who do it, but it is sin living in me that does it.

So I find this law at work: When I want to do good, evil is right there with me. For in my inner being I delight in God's law; but I see another law at work in the members of my body, waging war against the law of my mind and making me a prisoner of the law of sin at work within my members. What a wretched man I am! Who will rescue me from this body of death? *Thanks be to God—through Jesus Christ our Lord!*

Paul's Deliverer is the same as Peter's—and yours and mine.

J. M. Barrie, the creator of Peter Pan, picks up on Paul's theme: "The life of every man is a diary in which he means to write one story, and writes another." For most of us, our biographies are turning out far differently from—and quite inferior to—the success story we intended. While we agree with Barrie, though, we don't despair. Like Paul, we thank God for our deliverance "through Jesus Christ our Lord."

George Mueller, famed for his life of prayer and dependence on God as the head of his famous orphanage in Bristol, England, wrote one day in his journal, "This morning, I greatly dishonoured the Lord by irritability manifested towards my dear wife; and that, almost immediately after I had been on my knees before God, praising Him for having given me such a wife."[2]

I haven't written such words in my journal, but only because I don't have a journal. Mueller's confession caught my attention because as a younger Christian, I thought that if I could only attain real spirituality like that of, say, a George Mueller, my own battles with irritability (and other equally discouraging exhibits of a still-sinful character) would once and for all be over. Either I was wrong then or I am far from spirituality now!

Our unhappiness with our state of spiritual attainment will not be cured by simple acceptance of life's trials, as in Longfellow's famous lines: "Into each life some rain must fall, Some days must be dark and dreary."[3]

No, rainy days we can put up with. Dark and dreary thoughts, though, deliberate sins, stupid decisions, unfeeling and unthinking actions, these are what drive us crazy and make us wonder whether we'll ever get it right.

Nobody escapes. The sluggard could easily be written off. He just didn't try hard enough to achieve. But what about the achiever who did try hard enough, and who in fact has accomplished significant things, but who is still captive to a loose tongue, a slippery morality, a calloused heart, a quick temper, a debilitating habit? The Bible says, in one of its most obvious statements, "All have sinned and fall short of the glory of God" (Romans 3:23).

What then are we to do, to say, we who really do want to get it right?

The following suggestions are based on Scripture. I share them to help you, as they have helped me, to keep trying to get it right.

1) Don't *awfulize.*

Your mind—this is a mark of its perversity—leaps to believe the worst about your situation, about yourself in that situation. You've had troubles before, so when you see the cloud on the horizon you quickly conclude you're in for a thunderstorm. I've borrowed psychologist Albert Ellis's word here because it says it best. Things don't just look bad to us, they look *awful.* We imagine the absolute, overwhelming worst. Other psychologists call the tendency "catastrophizing." We aren't content with troubles. We have catastrophes! We even brag about them. "Nobody has had it as bad as I have." "Nobody has sinned as horribly, fallen so precipitously, messed up so completely, as I have." "God can't forgive me. I've gone too far."

We could use a little dose of Mark Twain's medicine here. Coming out of church one morning as it commenced raining heavily, his friend and fellow writer William Dean Howells asked, "Do you think it will stop?"

"It always has," answered Twain.

More than once I've held on to the old saying, "This too shall pass." One of the things I like about being in my sixth decade, as opposed to my younger years, is that I've lived long enough to see everything pass and to know that having survived so many other "awful" situations, I can survive the current one, also.

Maybe I've become so sanguine because Joy and I live in Arizona, the home state of Barry Goldwater, who must have had to apply some of this medicine back in the 1964 presidential campaign, when Lyndon Johnson's landslide victory buried him. Many years later he and Morris Udall, longtime member of the House of Representatives from Arizona (and also a former aspirant for the White House), were talking. The senator reminded the representative, "I got beat by Lyndon Johnson by sixteen million votes and you couldn't win a primary from Jimmy Carter. Between us, we've made Arizona the only state in the union where mothers don't tell their kids they can grow up to be President."[4]

But is it so *awful* not to be elected President? Both men survived their defeats and went on to respected post-campaign careers.

As far as Peter is concerned, Jesus' prediction of His suffering and death is just awful. Peter's concern is understandable. Humanly speaking, what Jesus is forecasting is as bad as it gets—until He adds, "and on the third day be raised to life." Peter doesn't hear that part. He's stuck on the usual. Usually when people die they stay dead. And that's awful. But Jesus faces His death with the assurance that after He has suffered and died there is more to come. He will return. When God is in control, the end of the story isn't the end of the story. So don't awfulize.

2) Trust some other people to be right.

Especially trust your best friends and loved ones to be right about *you*. The situation may look impossible, but that doesn't mean you aren't up to dealing with it. A minister, Robert J. Morgan, was discouraged by lack of growth in his church. The pressure on pastors these days to produce statistical growth is fierce. By numerical criteria, he wasn't succeeding. The numbers were against him. He was ready to turn in his letter of resignation. He would take down his ordination certificate and go into the feed and seed business. He convinced himself he was a failure. With his wife he flew to California from their home in Tennessee. Before taking the final step he had decided to seek counsel from Loren Lillistrand, a wise man whom a friend had recommended.

Loren asked him why he was so gripped by feelings of failure. "Does your wife think you've failed?" he asked.

"No."

"Does your church?"

"No. They love me."

"Do your friends think you've failed?"

"No, they think I'm doing pretty good."

"Does God think you've failed?"

"I don't think so."

"Then who thinks you're a failure?" he demanded.

"I do! I think I'm a failure!"

"So you know more than your wife, your church, your friends, and God—all put together? You may be smart," he explained, "but you're not *that* smart."[5]

Peter deserves his scolding as well. His heart is right, but his mouth is too quick. "Never, Lord! This shall never happen to you!" Who does he think he is, anyway? Does he know more than the one he has just called the Christ, "the Son of the living God"? He presumes to have better insight into Jesus' destiny than Jesus does.

He's disturbingly like the fellow whose wife said of him, "He's often wrong, but he's always sure." Nobody is more unpopular than the person who has the answer to every question, an opinion on every subject, an anecdote to top everybody else's. A little of what David Schwartz calls *conversation generosity* is called for, practicing restraint so that the other person can have the floor. After all, he just may be right.

3) Let go and hang on.

This recommendation has to do with trusting God. Peter can't accept God's plan for saving the world. He has been given insight into Jesus' personality and mission, but he has yet to learn to think in other worldly, Godly terms. He cannot imagine that God would let His own Son be abused and apparently defeated, any more than you and I can easily agree to God's allowing us to fail or suffer in order to accomplish some greater purpose of His own. We pray on the one hand, "Oh, God, lead me to do Your will," while on the other we resist that will if it goes contrary to what we have already decided is best for us.

We resist—and then wonder why our walk with the Lord seems so unsatisfactory. Why aren't things working out? Why does there seem to be so little joy for us?

Psychiatrist Scott Peck observes correctly that "the most common cause of depression is when a person is caught between the need to give up something and their will to hold on to it or their anger at having to give it up."[6] What has to be given up is the right to full control of our lives. To be a Christian is to surrender that control to Christ; to insist on doing things our way is to be in rebellion. What drains us of spiritual energy and prepares us for defeat is our stubborn insistence that we are letting God be Lord of our lives while at the same time we are hanging on for dear life to the controls.

"For dear life." There's the rub. We ought to know better, but we don't seem to. Consider the synonyms for "dear."

Cherished. We hang onto what we highly value, to the things, habits, attitudes that we can't imagine living without. They are certainly dearer to us than the new ways Christ teaches.

Favorite. They are our favorites because they seem to fit us; we've grown accustomed to their company.

Familiar. They are our cherished favorites because we picked them out ourselves. We understand them, are comfortable with them, and are not threatened by them.

Expensive, costly. Ah, here's another rub: what is dear is expensive. We pay a price. One of the things we hang onto for dear life is the right to control our own actions. We seldom count its cost, which is in relationships, peace of mind, acceptance by others, and harmony with God. Sometimes we must let go of what is dear to us because the price to be paid for hanging on is too expensive.

4) Remember: You have overcome many other problems.

Jesus has confidence in God's future for Him, a confidence that Peter lacks, because Jesus has already tested God's providence and found Him faithful. He can face the cross and the grave having already faced down the devil and his seductions. He has drawn on God's power to heal the sick and exorcise the demons. God's track record is a good one.

We tend to focus so much on our liabilities and disabilities that we discount our capabilities. Yet, as Paul testifies in 2 Corinthians 12, a thorn in the flesh may be the very means God uses to help us achieve something. Even the renowned author Somerset Maugham, whose point of view is decidedly not that of a Christian, reaches the same conclusion when, as an old man of eighty-six, he swears his greatest problem provided the impetus for his stunning success. Maugham stuttered. He credited his stammer, more than any other single thing in his life, for his achievements, and they were considerable: more than twenty books, thirty some plays, and scores of essays and short stories.

Think of Beethoven's deafness, Milton's blindness, Byron's clubfoot, Rodin's arthritis, Keller's blindness and deafness, Paul's poor health, Peter's impetuosity, Edison's dyslexia—to the naming of such names there is no end.

Think of Jesus' promise: "And surely I am with you always, to the very end of the age" (Matthew 28:20).

And of Paul's challenge: "If God is for us, who can be against us?" (Romans 8:31).

5) Believe that God will see you through.

Jesus trusts His safety to His Father. When the crisis comes, Matthew 26:39 records His personal desire ("My Father, if it is possible, may this cup be taken from me"), but He does not insist on taking over ("Yet not as I will, but as you will"). This trust explains His serenity when His disciples and friends seem to be losing theirs.

Jesus knows His Scriptures well. Undoubtedly He draws strength from passages like Moses' charge to Joshua as he prepared to turn over the reins of leadership. Joshua, too, would be facing fierce enemies, his decisions challenged by his own people, his mission threatened. So Moses exhorts him to "be strong and courageous, for you must go with this people into the land that the Lord swore to their forefathers to give them, and you must divide it among them as their inheritance. The Lord himself goes before you and will be with you; he will never leave you nor forsake you. Do not be afraid; do not be discouraged" (Deuteronomy 31:7, 8).

I wonder whether I've written a book in recent years that does not include Romans 8:28, the verse that has taken me through so many dark days: "And we know that in all things God works for the good of those who love him, who have been called according to his purpose."

That's promise enough, isn't it?

6) Look to tomorrow.

When discouragement strikes you, do what Jesus did. Look to tomorrow. "Let us fix our eyes on Jesus, the author and perfecter of our faith, who for the joy *set before him* endured the cross, scorning its shame, and sat down at the right hand of the throne of God" (Hebrews 12:2).

A long time ago I changed my style of pastoral counseling. Having studied psychology in the days when Freudian dogma, in its several mutations, was still the dominant orthodoxy, I began my counseling days by probing into the counselee's past, searching for reasons to explain current behavior. Such an exercise has value. After a few years, though, I concluded that while the past is helpful in explaining, it is of little value in correcting psychological problems. For wholeness, a good grasp on tomorrow is essential. What do you want to *do* tomorrow? Who do you want to *be* tomorrow? Where do you want to live in that tomorrow called eternity? What does your tomorrow require you to become today?

Jesus endured the cross because He kept his eye on tomorrow's joy.

George Bernard Shaw says many foolish things in his voluminous writings. And some very wise ones. Among the latter is what he has Don Juan, in his *Man and Superman*, declare: "I tell you that as long as I can conceive something better than myself, I cannot be easy until I am striving to bring it into existence or clearing the way for it."

Yes, it takes a long time to get it right, but as long as we can conceive something better than what we now are, and are striving to give that conception flesh and blood, our flesh and blood, we can endure the disappointments that life—and we—inflict on us. We can with Paul forget what lies behind and press on toward tomorrow. We can grow up. We can attain "to the whole measure of the fullness of Christ."

We can.

And by His grace, we shall.

Chapter 8

Casting Off Every Weight

Hebrews 12:1; Luke 17:3-5; 1 John 1:8-10; Philemon 8-22

In a study of victorious living, no greater challenge looms larger than facing—and facing down—the enemy called bitterness. Christian faith's motive force is not positive thinking, nor a heightened self-image, nor even Holy Spirit power. The most visible Christian sign is the cross, "the emblem of suffering and shame," as the old hymn asserts, but even more: the symbol of God's determination to save erring humanity through His forgiveness—and our own.

When the apostle Paul speaks of throwing off "everything that hinders [generality] and the sin [specific] that so easily entangles," he sounds like a coach instructing his cross-country team. Strip down, wear only the essentials. Reduce the resistance that slows you down. The essentials of the Christian race are faith in the Lord Jesus, fellowship in the body of Christ, energy from the Holy Spirit, instruction from God's Word, grace from the Father, and the like. What has to go are energy-sapping, soul-warping activities and attitudes that hobble the runner (see Colossians 3).

Nothing hobbles like refusing to forgive.

Failure to forgive another cuts off God's forgiveness, as Jesus warns in Matthew 6:12-15: "Forgive us our debts, *as* we also have forgiven our debtors."

"For if you forgive men when they sin against you, your heavenly Father will also forgive you. *But if you do not forgive men their sins, your Father will not forgive your sins.*"

To forgive is to leave it to God to make things right

"'Vengeance is mine, I will repay,' says the Lord." Sounds good, doesn't it? Until you actually try to forego the joy of revenge, that is. Then nothing else seems so sweet.

You may have seen the woman in the cartoon responding to her husband's plea, "Forgive you? For free?"[1] She has something else in mind. He did her wrong. He needs to pay for it. Call it tit for tat, or a tooth for a tooth, the spirit of revenge has long governed the affairs of men. And women. And men and women. It governs politics, business, sports, every arena of human relationships, as this popular story of some years ago illustrates. Its setting is the Korean war. Some American GIs employed a young Korean houseboy in their apartment. They had hired him to do their chores, but they retained him also for his entertainment value. He became the butt of their incessant and sometimes mean pranks. They nailed his shoes to the floor, smeared grease on the doorknobs, put a bucket of water over the door so he'd get drenched. What they could not do, however, was destroy his apparent placidity. He did not get angry, and he never tried to get even. They thought.

Eventually, his sweet spirit made them feel so guilty they had to apologize.

"You mean," he asked in initial unbelief, "no more shoes nailed to floor?"

"No, we're not going to do that any more," they promised.

"No more grease on doorknob?"

"No, we're not going to do that anymore, either."

"No more water over door?"

"No. No more."

"OK," he smiled, "No more spitting in soup."[2]

Dr. Susan Forward says there are "two facets to forgiveness: giving up the need for revenge, and absolving the guilty party of responsibility." In coming to grips with the subject, Dr. Forward reports she didn't have much trouble "accepting the idea that people have to let go of the need to get even. Revenge is a very normal but negative motivation. It bogs you down in obsessive fantasies about striking back to get satisfaction; it creates a lot of frustration and unhappiness; it works against your emotional well-being."

In other words, revenge is a "weight that so easily besets" us. But then she addresses the other facet: "absolving the guilty party of responsibility." That, she insists, you can't do.[3] Dr. Forward correctly identifies the aspect of forgiveness that trips us up. We can't stand it when we think someone who has offended us is getting away with it. We're afraid if we forgive we are telling the offender, "What you did is all right. Don't worry about it. It's nothing." But it's *not* nothing. It was wrong, and the culprit is still responsible.

We also fear that in forgiving we may be absolving the offender of responsibility by taking it on ourselves. "I must have done something wrong. It must have been my fault after all. Therefore, I forgive you." Thus reasons the enabler, the codependent.

Forgiveness involves my holding no bitterness against you for what you did. I will not allow something in the past to control my attitudes and behavior in the present. I will therefore remember your offense no more. I manage my attitude, not you. Your misconduct toward me cannot force me to retaliate in any way. I will not even resent you. I forgive you and free myself.

Forgiving is taking another at his word

"So watch yourselves. If your brother sins, rebuke him, and if he repents, forgive him. If he sins against you seven times in a day, and seven times comes back to you and says, 'I repent,' forgive him."

When Jesus' apostles heard this teaching, they implored him, "Increase our faith!" (Luke 17:3-5). Forgiveness is so radically different from typical human responses to sins against us that only a mature faith in God can achieve it.

To forgive
is to become honest about yourself

At the root of bitterness is self-deception. Although the offended speak of "getting even," that isn't what they really want, because "getting even" connotes equality, and they don't feel equal, but superior. The offended—listen to their language—don't really want anyone to consider them somehow the same as the offender. That's never good enough. "How dare that low life treat *me* like this? What have I ever done to deserve this?" Vengeance is the dream of the proud.

John speaks in general terms about sin, and in general we can agree with him: "If we claim to be without sin, we deceive ourselves and the truth is not in us. . . . If we claim we have not sinned, we make him out to be a liar and his word has no place in our lives" (1 John 1:8, 10).

Paul comes closer to home when he exhorts us to "bear with each other and forgive whatever grievances you may have against one another. Forgive as the Lord forgave you" (Colossians 3:13).

It's that last sentence that should stop us short. To forgive as the Lord forgave me. . . . "But, but," I sputter, "I haven't ever done anything as bad as what *he/she* did to me." Perhaps. Yet if John is right, we are still guilty of sinning, disappointing God, being less than thoroughly Christian. In God's eyes, how different do you suppose you and your offender look?

Jesus addresses this disparity between our self-perception and our perception of others in His famous parable of the tax collector and the Pharisee:

> To some who were confident of their own righteousness and looked down on everybody else, Jesus told this parable: "Two men went up to the temple to pray, one a Pharisee and the other a tax collector. The Pharisee stood up and prayed about himself: 'God, I thank you that I am not like other men—robbers, evildoers, adulterers—or even like this tax collector. I fast twice a week and give a tenth of all I get.'

"But the tax collector stood at a distance. He would not even look up to heaven, but beat his breast and said, 'God, have mercy on me, a sinner.'

"I tell you that this man, rather than the other, went home justified before God. For everyone who exalts himself will be humbled, and he who humbles himself will be exalted" (Luke 18:9-14).

Jesus implies that the more righteous we feel, the more deceived we may be about ourselves. Remember that in the eyes of Jesus' contemporaries, nobody was more contemptible than a tax collector, and no one more righteous than a Pharisee. But God, who sees the inner workings of the heart, has a different perspective. The right one.

Although we may be humble enough to recognize the sinner in ourselves, we still find forgiving a trial. It's never over with. When we think we've dealt with an issue and resolved it once and for all, it pops up again. C. S. Lewis, always an honest student of spiritual values, describes the difficulty well: "For we find that the work of forgiveness has to be done over and over again. We forgive, we mortify our resentment; a week later some chain of thought carries us back to the original offense and we discover the old resentment blazing away as if nothing had been done about it at all. We need to forgive our brother seventy times seven not only for 490 offenses but for one offense."[4]

This incompetence in forgiving exposes our pretensions of moral superiority. If we're so spiritual, why is forgiveness so incessantly difficult? If forgiveness eludes us, how can we claim to be better than the one who has wronged us? And if we are no better than he is, what right have we to wreak any vengeance?

Many years before Christ taught us to forgive, the Greek philosopher Epictetus was teaching very much the same thing:

> Every matter has two handles, one of which will bear taking hold of, the other not. If thy brother sin against thee, lay not hold of the matter by this, that he sins against thee; for by this handle the matter will not bear taking hold of. But rather lay hold of it by this, that he is thy brother, thy born mate; and thou wilt take hold of it by what will bear handling."[5]

Chuck Colson tells of an honest judge who found his spiritual brother in prison. Colson had taken a group of Christians into the Indiana State Penitentiary to minister to inmates on death row. When their allotted time was up and they were checking out, he discovered one of his group missing. He and a guard hurried back to hunt for him. He was discovered deep in conversation with a prisoner. Colson scolded him for violating their agreement with the warden.

"You don't understand," he explained. "This is James Brewer. He's condemned to die. I'm Judge Clement. I'm the one who sentenced him. Since that time we've both become Christians, and we need some time to confess and to forgive each other."[6]

Judge and criminal on equal ground. Neither could have become a Christian without admitting sin. Each had hurt fellow human beings and affronted God. Neither was pure. In becoming honest with God, they could become reconciled to each other.

In his letter to Philemon, the apostle Paul draws an analogy between Onesimus's literal slavery and his own incarceration as a "prisoner of Christ," a phrase used three times in this brief letter. Elsewhere (Romans 1:1; 1 Corinthians 7:22; Galatians 1:10; Ephesians 6:6; Philippians 1:1; Colossians 4:12) Paul commonly refers to himself and other believers as slaves or servants of Christ, and as prisoners of Christ. In a very real sense, this apostle has no difficulty forgiving Onesimus, the runaway slave; he's a slave himself. So, for that matter, is Philemon, Onesimus's master, whom Paul urges to forgive his errant servant: ". . . have him back for good—no longer as a slave, but . . . as a dear brother . . . welcome him as you would welcome me," Paul urges. In the world, they are master and slave. In Christ, they are fellow sinners, fellow slaves. One is not superior to the other, so one cannot withhold forgiveness from the other.

To forgive is to act in spite of, not because of

Remember the woman who didn't want to forgive her husband "for free"? She may not have liked the conditions, but she was beginning to catch on to the nature of forgiveness.

It is offered *in spite of* the gravity of the offense and not because of any compensation offered.

Without the "in spite of" character of the gospel, we would have no hope. Our prayer is as old as Moses': "In accordance with *your* great love, forgive the sin of these people, just as you have pardoned them from the time they left Egypt until now" (Numbers 14:19).

Moses was counting on the same grace of God we depend on. He knew God's forgiveness is independent of anything we have done or can do. It is not because of our contrition or our good works or anything else but His nature that we have hope of reconciliation with Him. "God's forgiveness," John Krumm writes,

> is independent of anything we do, even of self-accusation and self-humiliation. . . . Forgiveness creates repentance. . . . God does not offer men the forgiveness of the Cross after they have come to him in contrition and remorse; he holds out to them the forgiveness of the Cross as an initial gesture in the hope that it may lead to a recognition of the depth of their sin and make the path of repentance not a crushing self-humiliation but a self-forgetful opening of the heart to divine love.[7]

Thus Jesus told His disciples in that moving last supper experience, "This is my blood of the covenant, which is poured out for many for the forgiveness of sins." We hang on to these words today, though they were spoken nearly two thousand years ago. His blood was given for our forgiveness *before* we needed it. On the Day of Pentecost Peter did not hesitate to offer "forgiveness of your sins . . . and . . . the gift of the Holy Spirit" to those who would repent and be baptized. God, he knew, had already made provision for their forgiveness. They could be assured of this even before they took the step of expressing their contrition in repentance and baptism.

Paul later picked up on this same theme, making the same promise: "In him we have redemption through his blood, the forgiveness of sins, in accordance with the riches of God's grace" (Ephesians 1:7).

All this leads us to examine our interpersonal relationships. If we are to forgive as God has forgiven us, then we pardon those who have hurt us in spite of the hurt. We no longer say, "Sure I'll forgive _____, if only he'll do this or say that." Nor do we say, "Because you have shown adequate remorse for your heinous deed and have promised to make it up to me, I will forgive you." No, the Christian takes the initiative: "I forgive you, whether you do whatever I think you should or don't. My attitude toward you is not governed by your meeting certain conditions I lay down, but by my determination that nothing in me will be liable for maintaining the breach between us."

Dr. Scott Peck, whose psychological insights often test our complacency, doesn't deny the inevitability of our anger, but warns against hanging on to it, because beyond a certain point, he insists, you hurt yourself.

> The process of forgiveness—indeed the chief reason for forgiveness—is selfish. The reason to forgive others is not for their sake. They are not likely to know that they need to be forgiven. They're not likely to remember their offense. . . . The reason to forgive is for your own sake. For your own health. Because beyond that point needed for healing, if we hold on to our anger, we stop growing and our souls begin to shrivel."[8]

So we forgive, in spite of.

To forgive is to leave the past for the present and future

The "in spite of" spirit liberates me from bondage to past behavior, either yours or mine. To set preconditions, the "because of" mentality, boxes me in and makes me dependent on your willingness or unwillingness to meet the conditions. Today is therefore held in thrall to yesterday, and I don't even know what I'll do or feel tomorrow, because I have to wait until I see what you're going to do first. It's a form of mental and emotional slavery.

Arthur H. Dauer, a fifty-one-year-old Jupiter, Florida, stockbroker, finally made up his mind to shake off the shackles of a sin committed in his long-ago childhood. He took out a seventy-dollar newspaper advertisement to confess to wrongly accusing a six-year-old classmate of being a thief. When they were in the first grade he accused her of stealing a penny's worth of peanut butter and crackers. This was in 1938, forty-six years earlier.

"Viola, I am sorry," read the 3" x 3" ad in *Trenton Times*. "In the McClellan School in East Trenton in the school year 1937-38, we were in Miss Cunningham's first-grade class. I was forced to accuse you of stealing a one-cent peanut butter and saltine sandwich. I did not think you were guilty—and I have always been sorry. Arthur H. Dauer."

The snack his mother had prepared for him disappeared. The teacher had him smell the breath of each classmate. He pointed the finger at Viola, even though her breath didn't carry the telltale odor.

"I remember the girl cried, got very upset and didn't come back to school for several days." He said she was very quiet, very meek. "I can picture her face in front of me like it was yesterday."

When he took out the ad, Dauer didn't know whether she was alive, or whether anyone would read it. "I feel better. I don't know if she'll read it, if she's alive, or if anyone will read it. I just know that I feel better about it. I've just been looking at life and thinking about things I wish I had done differently."[9]

In this case, Dauer was the guilty party. I wish we knew Viola's part of the story. How long did it take her to forgive him. Or did she? What would have happened if she had carried her sense of injustice for forty years, as he had carried his sense of guilt? What would it have done to her joy of life, to her sense of fair play, to her courage in social intercourse?

Marie Balter provides an answer. If ever there was an abused child, Marie was the one. Misdiagnosed as schizophrenic, Marie was locked up in the Danvers, Massachusetts, State Hospital for seventeen years. What the officials thought was schizophrenia was really depression, which she had every reason to experience. Marie was the illegitimate daughter of an alcoholic mother who put her in a foster home when she was five. Then she was adopted by a Gloucester couple whose harsh discipline included locking her in the cellar, among similar atrocities.

Released from the hospital in 1964, she returned to school

and eventually attained her master's degree from Harvard.
Then she returned to the scene of her long incarceration to
serve the needs of the patients there. Her story was the basis
of a 1986 TV movie starring Marlo Thomas.

What does this remarkable woman say about the injustice
of those lost years? The bitterness you might expect is absent.
"I wouldn't have grown one bit if I didn't learn how to forgive. If you don't forgive your parents or your children or
yourself, you don't get beyond that anger. Forgiving is a way
of reaching out from a bad past and heading out to a more
positive future.[10]

That positive future is forever denied to one who will not
forgive until there is retribution, or revenge. To forgive is to
be released from the past, set free for the future.

To forgive is to unclutter your memory

The past we remember may not be the past that was, anyway. Memory cannot be trusted as the final authority. As
John Barlow, songwriter for The Grateful Dead, asserts
"History is what you remember, and if you don't think it's
being revised all the time, you haven't paid enough attention
to your own memory. When you remember something, you
don't remember the thing itself—you just remember the last
time you remembered it."[11]

The longer you nurse a grudge because of some real or al-
leged fault, the more times you rehearse the event, the more
likely you are to change some of the details, color some of
your interpretation, and distort your recall. In time, the
words you remember your offender speaking, the offensive
acts you so deeply resent, may not in fact have been spoken
or done, at least not as you think they were. What you are
savoring is not the impression of the event, but images seen
through a glass darkly, and your accusations tell more about
the person you now are than they do about the persons you
and your offender were then.

Norman Vincent Peale tells of a woman who came forward
after worship service one Sunday morning. "Why do I always
itch?" she asked, showing him the offensive rash on her
arm—which he couldn't see. As he probed her memory with

her to ascertain the source of her discomfort, he learned of her virulent hatred of her sister. She was convinced the sister had cheated her out of part of their father's estate. He checked with her doctor to see what insight he could shed on the mystery. He understood her plight completely. "She has mental eczema," he explained. "She itches not in her body, but in her mind; and it's that old hate that is causing it. Cure her of that, and she should be a well person."

Dr. Peale worked with her, explaining the "mental-spiritual mechanism" that governed her problem. He was able to lead her to forgive her sister. In time, the itching stopped.[12]

"To err is human," Alexander Pope observes, and "to forgive divine." To forgive is also human. It's a must for victory in Jesus.

Chapter 9

Keep On Keeping On

Acts 26:1-32; 2 Timothy 4:6-8

I wonder whether today's high school students recognize the name of John Paul Jones. When my generation was young, we were fed stories of American heroes. We were taught to glory in our nation's past, to take pride in the valiant souls who defied death to guarantee a free America. One of those heroes was John Paul Jones, who more than two centuries ago gained a certain immortality by shouting to the apparently victorious British, "I have not yet begun to fight!"

As captain of the *Bonhomme Richard,* Jones learned of a British convoy transporting a large number of merchant men. He caught up with it at sunset on September 23, 1779 off Flamborough Head on the Yorkshire Coast. It was some convoy. Forty-one ships were escorted by the powerful new British two-decker *Serapis,* which boasted fifty guns, including twenty eighteen-pounders, far superior to Jones's forty guns with six eighteen-pounders.

The two warships opened fire and bombarded one another nonstop for the next three hours. Then they closed to a distance within pistol shot. The *Serapis* scored a hit to the powder charges on the *Richard's* gun deck, killing many of the gunners and silencing Jones's heaviest guns. Barbara Tuchman describes the scene:

> The Richard's decks were on fire and her hull taking in water.
> With his ship faced with the danger of sinking, the Richard's chief
> gunner screamed to the Serapis, "Quarter! Quarter! for God's sake!"
> Jones hurled a pistol at the man, felling him. But the cry had been
> heard by Pearson, the Serapis's commander, who called, "Do you
> ask for quarter?" Through the clash of battle, gunshot and crackle
> of fire the famous reply came faintly back to him: "I have not yet
> begun to fight!"[1]

Jones commandeered a nine-pounder whose gun crew had been killed or wounded, loaded and fired it at the *Serapis's* mainmast. The mast toppled. Pearson was beaten. He hauled down his red ensign, signaling surrender.

The battle was over. On the *Richard's* quarterdeck, Pearson handed his sword to Jones just as the *Serapis's* mainmast crashed over the side.

It was an expensive battle, costing many lives, sinking the victorious *Bonhomme Richard* the next day, and badly crippling the *Serapis,* in which the triumphant Jones headed for Holland, arriving ten days later. In the story of the American Revolutionary War, the battle of these ships is but a footnote. But Jones's famous words have never died. They signify courage, daring, and determination in the face of insuperable odds. They breathed hope in a hopeless situation.

In a much less dramatic way, France's General de Castelnau's remark following a devastating loss to invading Germans at Morhange in World War I conveys the same grim determination. His son had just been killed in battle. When word of his death reached his father, the general's staff tried to express their sympathy. Then, after a pause, he said, in a phrase that later rallied Frenchmen as Jones's had rallied Americans, "We will continue, gentlemen."[2] That was it. It was enough.

"I have not yet begun to fight."

"We will continue, gentlemen."

"I pray God that not only you but all who are listening to me today may become what I am, except for these chains."

The apostle Paul's words (Acts 26:29) are at home in this company, aren't they? Facing King Agrippa as a political prisoner, Paul doesn't back down an inch. Agrippa hears no apology from the embattled preacher, no compromising of

his position, no plea for clemency in exchange for recanting.
Not only does he express no regrets, he uses this unusual
setting as an opportunity to present the gospel's claims to
the king.

"Do you think that in such a short time you can persuade
me to be a Christian?" the startled monarch asks him.

We've already heard Paul's answer. He regrets nothing but
his chains. He wants everyone, even the king, to "become
what I am" (Acts 26:28, 29). His confidence is unshaken, his
satisfaction in the Lord complete.

We marvel at the boldness of these men. You and I have
no such tale to tell—at least I don't. By comparison, our trials
seem small, even petty, yet they are sometimes enough, more
than enough, to tempt us to quit this Christian pilgrimage,
to find some easier route through life.

Unlike Jones, we whimper to a friend, "I want out. There's
no more fight left in me. It's not worth it."

We alter General de Castelnau's words only so slightly: "We
will *not* continue, gentlemen."

And we soften Paul's: "I pray God that *no one* will have to
endure what I've been going through."

So what do you do when you're at the end of your rope?
Robert Schuller likes to advise us to tie a knot in it and hang
on. That sounds good enough, until you try to figure out
how to tie the knot while dangling weakly at the rope's end.
Then what?

In a way, Schuller's advice is similar to that old joke about
the Wall Street advisor who was describing to a prospective
client how the stock market works. The way to make money,
he solemnly intoned, is to buy low and sell high. But if your
stock goes down? Then don't buy, the broker blandly re-
torted.

Solutions "after the fact" are as plentiful as they are use-
less. When you are actually at the end of the rope is not the
time to be worrying about tying the knot. You tie it in the
beginning, before you take hold of the rope.

The captain, the general, and the apostle had one thing in
common: they were so filled with their mission they could
not be stopped, not by a sea battle, not by a death, not by

imprisonment and an uncertain future. Their perseverance in the face of adversity gave them their victory.

Let's look more closely at the apostle's court appearance to find clues to what keeps him keeping on.

Vision

Paul's vision accounts for his tenacity. "I was not disobedient to the vision from heaven," he tells Agrippa. Once he knew where he had to go, he did not deviate from the charge the Lord gave him. Three times in the book of Acts Paul recounts the story of how the Lord called him on the road to Damascus by a blinding light from Heaven. The experience transformed him from Christian persecutor to Christian apostle. If ever tempted to retreat, he remembered the light.

In 1831 one of America's great visionaries, William Lloyd Garrison, published the first issue of his abolitionist journal, *The Liberator,* destined to become the movement's most influential publication. The paper came out even though the publisher was broke. To buy more paper and ink, he sold his bed and slept on the floor. To keep his paper going, he trimmed his diet so severely that pounds fell from his already thin frame. His project cost him everything. His enemies shunned and heaped abuse upon him, once dragging him through the streets of Boston by a halter around his neck. In spite of everything they did to him, his *Liberator* kept appearing. In the end, slavery was abolished.

"My country is the World. My countrymen are mankind," declared his masthead on *The Liberator.* All of mankind, he meant, not just those who shared his skin color. His tenacity breathed through everything he did. "I am in earnest," he declared. "I will not equivocate, I will not excuse, I will not retreat a single step, and I will be heard."[3] He was.

Another great practical idealist, England's General William Booth, founder of the Salvation Army, kept his vision even when he lost his sight. His son Bramwell had to break the news to him that he was indeed going blind, that the affliction troubling his eyes would not be temporary.

"You mean that I am blind?"

"I fear you must contemplate that."

"I shall never see your face again?"

"No," said Bramwell, "not in this world."

The old spiritual warrior's hand then grasped his son's: "Bramwell, I have done what I could for God and the people with my eyes; now I shall do what I can for God and the people without my eyes."[4]

He would not be "disobedient to the heavenly vision."

Confidence

The unswerving determination of a Booth in blindness or a Garrison under attack or an apostle Paul before King Herod Agrippa is more than personal stubbornness. The vision gives it birth, but unwavering confidence in the vision keeps it strong. In spite of opposition, hardship, persecution, fatigue —in spite of everything—these men knew that they had given themselves to something true and honorable. They were men of integrity. Once convinced they were under God's orders, they would not be moved.

They are like William Penn, tossed into London Tower for his unpopular religious convictions, who vowed, "My prison shall be my grave before I will budge a jog; for I owe my conscience to no mortal man."[5]

Such words take us back to Job, who vows (in the *King James* translation), "Though he slay me, yet will I trust in him" (13:15). The Alexander Pope translation packs even more punch: "He may slay me, I'll not quaver. I will defend my conduct to his face." The first sounds like submission, but the latter more like defiance. Job sees himself as a man of integrity who has not wronged God. He can defend himself before accusers, even God, if God should charge him.

Paradoxically, his confidence in God enables him to stand against God—or at least those who accuse him in the name of God. He knows God's will and has lived according to it all his life. He will not be bullied into renouncing his conduct when everything in him cries against the injustice of his plight. He has not been disobedient, either, to his "heavenly vision."

You may be more like me than like Job. Don't you wish we could claim never to have wavered, never to have been disobedient? I can't. My confidence in myself has often slackened. My confidence in God has, to say the least, been stronger at some times than others. Unable to stand with Paul against the authorities, or with Garrison against enemies, or with Booth against physical infirmities, or with Job against disaster, the best I could muster has been a saving desire to be rescued from my weakness. "Create in me a pure heart, O God, and renew a steadfast spirit within me" is the psalmist's prayer (51:10), and mine. It's the petition of a man who knows his own strength and the insufficiency thereof, who grasps Peter's benediction and claims its promise: "And the God of all grace, who called you to his eternal glory in Christ, after you have suffered a little while, will himself restore you and make you strong, firm and steadfast" (1 Peter 5:10).

In that promise we can take confidence.

Discipline

Neither vision nor confidence by themselves can keep us keeping on. The more glorious the vision, the more arduous the fulfillment. The harder the journey to victory, the more seductive the temptations to take an easier detour. "All our final resolutions are made in a state of mind which is not going to last," Marcel Proust has written. What seems so doable on the spiritual mountaintop seems impossible in the doldrums. If we let our feelings have their sway, no heavenly vision can sustain us. Peter states it more strongly. The problem is not our feelings, but God's enemy. He'll do what he must to thwart God's purposes in our lives: "Be self-controlled and alert. Your enemy the devil prowls around like a roaring lion looking for someone to devour. Resist him, standing firm in the faith, because you know that your brothers throughout the world are undergoing the same kind of sufferings" (1 Peter 5: 8, 9).

Such tribulation is universal. What is less universal is victory over tribulation. For that, discipline ("be self-controlled and alert") is required. Peter implies that the devil *can* be resisted—and that we are not alone in our struggle against him.

So like Paul we "buffet our bodies," resisting the devil's lures, overcoming the flesh's temptations, finding the will to keep going when everything in us cries out to quit. Charles Barkley, the heart of the Phoenix Suns' basketball team, punished his aging body season after season to lead his team to championship playoffs. His fans would ask as each year's play drew to a close, "Will he be back? Can his body take another season of it?" Several years earlier, Barkley revealed what kept him going. "Even the healthiest body can survive only about forty NBA games," he said. "For the next twenty games, an NBA player exists on will."[6]

Only a disciplined will can keep the tired body going. Without it, surrender is certain.

The popular term lately for that surrender is "burnout." That's what Martin Luther King called it at a conference in 1964, at the height of his struggle for civil rights in America. Believing "we have just so much strength in us," King described the onset of burnout as giving and giving until:

> we have less and less and less—and after a while, at a certain point, we're so weak and worn, we hoist up the flag of surrender. We surrender to the worst side of ourselves, and then we display that to others. We surrender to self-pity and to spite and to morose self-preoccupation. If you want to call it depression or burnout, well, all right. If you want to call it the triumph of sin—when our goodness has been knocked out from under us, well, all right. Whatever we say or think, this is arduous duty, doing this kind of work; to live out one's idealism brings with it hazards.[7]

Yet so vital is that disciplined dedication to idealism that John Milton, writing in the seventeenth century, believed "The flourishing and decaying of all civil societies, all the moments and turnings of human occasions are moved to and fro upon the axle of discipline."[8]

Societies cannot survive without it, movements falter without it, and individuals burn out when it does not accompany the vision, no matter how confident the visionary is of his heavenly calling.

Hope

But no one can apply the rigors of discipline without the rewards of hope. Hope permeates Paul's defense before Agrippa. He has had God's help "to this very day" and counts on it for whatever his future holds. His letters pulsate to the rhythms of hope. "For I am already being poured out like a drink offering, and the time has come for my departure. I have fought the good fight, I have finished the race, I have kept the faith. Now there is in store for me the crown of righteousness, which the Lord, the righteous Judge, will award to me on that day—and not only to me, but also to all who have longed for his appearing" (2 Timothy 4:6-8).

His suffering is intense, his victories hard won, his God-given assignment completed. He has been faithful. He can now look forward to "the crown" soon to be awarded him. He has sacrificed much, but never in vain. He believed, as he wrote to the Corinthians, that for the steadfast in the work of the Lord, "your labor in the Lord is not in vain" (1 Corinthians 15:58). Nor is it, though it might appear to be at times, solitary. The Lord who calls also sustains—through everything.

"In all these things we are more than conquerors through him who loved us. For I am convinced that neither death nor life, neither angels nor demons, neither the present nor the future, nor any powers, neither height nor depth, nor anything else in all creation, will be able to separate us from the love of God that is in Christ Jesus our Lord" (Romans 8:37-39).

"Our hope is in the Lord" is a theme song for achieving Christians. Aware of our inherent weakness, we hang on to the hope that is laid before us. Knowing nothing can separate us from the Source of our hope, we are emboldened to try to achieve goals unimaginable on our own.

Roger Bannister's triumph in track has become a staple illustration for ministers who are trying to preach hope into their timid congregations. The English physician broke the four-minute mile, a feat that seemed impossible until he did it in 1954. Men had been racing against one another from the beginning of athletic contests. Why did it take so long to achieve this speed? Bannister believed that men had failed to break this record simply because people didn't think it could be done. In 1886 a man named Walker ran the mile in four minutes, twelve and three-quarters seconds, a world record. Thirty-seven years later Paavo Nurmi set a new record, four minutes, ten and three-quarters seconds, shaving two seconds off the earlier one. Thirty-one years after Nurmi's feat, Bannister proved the mile could be run in less than four minutes. Since then, dozens of competitors have done so. What has made the difference? Bannister offered this simple hypothesis: the psychology of racing changed. Once the barrier was broken, serious runners have had reason to hope they, too, could do it.

Reason to hope.

In matters large and small, reason to hope keeps us going.

For the rest of our lives, Joy and I will probably remember 1994 as the worst year of our lives. We've known many heartaches and losses, but when our son took his own life in May of that year, we grieved as never before. The months following were in many ways a nightmare, despite the best ministrations of our loved ones. With the illogical minds of the mourning, we earnestly wished that the tragedy had not happened.

For a close friend of ours, 1993 was his family's year of misery. Each of their two daughters, their only children, announced they were divorcing their husbands. Divorce so closely resembles death that Joy and I readily identified with their heartache. Our friends were miserable. He wrote about their year of misery in this poem.

Annus Miserabilis 1993

I shall not grieve your passing, Annus Miserabilis,
For I have grieved enough for one year.
Your Alpha and Omega was Death.
And Death made me the quiet orphan,
Quiet, for three-scored orphans cannot name
Their loneliness such.

I shall not grieve your passing, Annus Miserabilis,
For you could not bear our family happiness.
Your serpent, Alienation, came to our garden,

And took from us two sons, our daughters' gifts to us.
Flawed though they were (and aren't we all)
They loved and were loved. And in their dispatching
We have lost something of what we had in our daughters.

I shall not grieve your passing, Annus Miserabilis,
For you have not the power to take from us
The One who makes all things new,
Who stands triumphant at open grave,
Who waits in love for loved ones wandering,
Who groans with us, His creation.

Annus Miserabilis, your time was short.
Your trophies did not include our family treasure.
The love we bear to one another is still safe,
At times groping for words,
But always waiting patiently to serve.
If you have served us, it is to know better
Him who gives us not *annia* but *aeternitas*,
Not *miserabilis* but *redemptio*.

—Laterum Structor
January 2, 1994

Our friends took their solace where we found ours, not in today but in eternity, not in feelings but in fact. They felt their loss beyond word's telling, but they endured because of the fact that theirs is a redeeming, sustaining Lord. Thanks to Him, they were able to keep on keeping on.

Gratitude

Thanks to Him. Sooner or later, we return to thanksgiving. Hope looks forward and sees a reason to keep on. Gratitude looks backward and, because of so much already received, has every expectation of more to be given, and so keeps on.

"But I have had God's help to this very day," Paul tells the king. Implicit in the acknowledgment is the gratitude. His enemies tried to get him, but God prevented them.

These are not idle words. Think of what the man had suffered:

Five times I received from the Jews the forty lashes minus one.
Three times I was beaten with rods,
once I was stoned,
three times I was shipwrecked,
I spent a night and a day in the open sea,
I have been constantly on the move.
I have been in danger from rivers,
in danger from bandits,
in danger from my own countrymen,
in danger from Gentiles;
in danger in the city,
in danger in the country,
in danger at sea;
and in danger from false brothers.
I have labored and toiled and have often gone without sleep;
I have known hunger and thirst and have often gone without
    food;
I have been cold and naked.
Besides everything else, I face daily the pressure of my concern
    for all the churches.   2 Corinthians 11:24-28

What would James offer as the final word about Paul's
trials? Here it is:

Consider it pure joy, my brothers, whenever you face trials of
many kinds, because you know that the testing of your faith develops perseverance. Perseverance must finish its work so that you may
be mature and complete, not lacking in anything (James 1:2-4).

Paul is of a similar opinion as he writes:

Let the peace of Christ rule in your hearts, since as members of
one body you were called to peace. And be thankful. Let the word of
Christ dwell in you richly as you teach and admonish one another
with all wisdom, and as you sing psalms, hymns and spiritual songs
with gratitude in your hearts to God. And whatever you do, whether
in word or deed, do it all in the name of the Lord Jesus, giving
thanks to God the Father through him (Colossians 3:15-17).

And in 1 Corinthians:

But thanks be to God! He gives us the victory through our Lord
Jesus Christ. Therefore, my dear brothers, stand firm. Let nothing
move you. Always give yourselves fully to the work of the Lord,
because you know that your labor in the Lord is not in vain (1
Corinthians 15:57, 58).

Chapter 10

Remember
Who You Are

Galatians 3:26-29; 1 Corinthians 10:11-13;
Hebrews 4:15; 12:1, 2; Matthew 4:1-11

Victory assumes an opponent. You are victorious *over* or *against* someone or something. Victorious living is accomplished in the face of temptation, confrontation, or antagonism. So far in this study we have been taking this fact for granted. Now it's time to look more directly at our battle with temptation—and the tempter. In the Bible, that tempter is Satan, the enemy (Matthew 13:25, 28, 39), and deceiver (Revelation 20:10), who is the prince of this world (John 12:31; 14:30; 16:11) but who acts like a "roaring lion looking for someone to devour," (1 Peter 5:8).

Satan's strategy is simple. He "does not here fill us with hatred of God," Dietrich Bonhoeffer has helpfully pointed out, "but with forgetfulness of God."[1] If we can be made to forget who God is, or who we His children are, Satan can have his way with us.

Satan is strong—but the unforgetful Christian is stronger (Ephesians 6:11; 1 Corinthians 10:13). With the arm of the Lord as his strength, he can fend off the devil (James 4:7).

God's Word pledges that "the one who is in you is greater than the one who is in the world" (1 John 4:4).

The enemy is powerful, but the mindful Christian, through the strength of the Holy Spirit, is stronger still. The observation of Brother Julian of Norwich is worth recalling: "He [the Lord] said not: Thou shall not be troubled—thou shalt not be tempted—thou shalt not be distressed. But He said: Thou shalt not be overcome."[2]

But if you would resist the devil, you dare not ever forget who you are.

You are a child of God

Who are you? God's child! Scripture declares this almost unbelievable fact in a number of passages. Here's one of the best: "You are all sons of God through faith in Christ Jesus, for all of you who were baptized into Christ have clothed yourselves with Christ. There is neither Jew nor Greek, slave nor free, male nor female, for you are all one in Christ Jesus. If you belong to Christ, then you are Abraham's seed, and heirs according to the promise" (Galatians 3:26-29).

The apostle Paul's rhetoric soars even higher in Ephesians 1:4, 5: "For he chose us in him before the creation of the world to be holy and blameless in his sight. In love he predestined us to be adopted as his sons through Jesus Christ, in accordance with his pleasure and will."

The apostle's doctrine is the Christian's hope: You belong! You are a valued member of the family of God; you are a chosen (adopted) child. Everything the Father wants you to have is yours, including power over the devil himself. Claim it.

William Barclay, whose Bible teaching has been an inspiration and encouragement to millions of Christians, found himself severely tested when his own daughter was killed in a boating accident. It could not have been easy for him to carry on his ministry. Yet he could write:

> Temptation is not meant to make us fall; it is meant to confront us with a situation out of which we emerge stronger than we were. Temptation is not the penalty of manhood; it is the glory of manhood.

> Because I believe this, I believe that pain and suffering are never the will of God for his children.[3]

He wrote those words as he was discussing God's testing of Abraham (Genesis 22). God was *testing* Abraham, Barclay insists, not *tempting* him. Barclay would never allow anyone to say to him, as he made his pastoral visits among his stricken people, "This is the will of God." His personal faith was challenged once on a British Broadcasting Company interview with David Winter. His host wanted to know how he had come to his understanding of God's will in our lives and his belief that the miracles of Jesus were recorded to convince us not only that Jesus did things nineteen hundred years ago but does things today.

> I told him the truth. I told him that some years ago our twenty-one year old daughter and the lad to whom she would some day have been married were both drowned in a yachting accident. I said that God did not stop that accident at sea, but he did still the storm in my own heart, so that somehow my wife and I came through that terrible time still on our own two feet.[4]

What most interests this Bible scholar is the Lord's power at work within us today. No, "interests" is too weak a word. It's the knowledge of God's power in us that sustains, emboldens, and inspires him. Not power by itself, but the believer's certainty that God wants good for His children. As Professor Barclay puts it, "Pain and suffering are never the will of God *for his children*."

With that understanding, Barclay would undoubtedly have agreed with John Vianney that "the greatest of all evils is *not* to be tempted, because there are then grounds for believing that the devil looks upon us as his property."[5] The devil, not God, is behind the evil we experience. God, not the devil, works in the untoward circumstances to bring good out of them (Romans 8:28 again), to strengthen His children through them. A friend of novelist Flannery O'Connor would have *amen*ed Vianney, even to the point of criticizing the Lord's Prayer. "Imagine asking not to be led into temptation! We should ask to be led into temptations so that we could grow strong and overcome them!"[6]

That is a risk I'm unwilling to take. Past temptations have proved my personal weakness more than my strength. Yet there is some truth in these protestations, isn't there? John Milton scoffed at "cloistered virtue," that piety that can boast it has never been sullied by temptation because it hides from all encounters with the world. Such virtue isn't virtue at all. No loving parent locks her child in the house indefinitely in order to keep the child safe from all harm. No, maturation demands engagement with the world. Without the struggle there is no victory. But the child draws courage from knowing that the loving—and stronger—parent is near at hand, watching, making certain the child is not going out too far or in too deep.

The first lesson in dealing with temptation, then, is to remember who you are.

You are a vulnerable child of God

The second point to remember is that you are not invincible, even as a child of God. Your defenses can be penetrated, your resolve weakened. C. S. Lewis offers a heartening word here:

> I know all about the despair of overcoming chronic temptations. It is not serious, provided self-offended petulance, annoyance at breaking records, impatience etc. don't get the upper hand. No amount of falls will really undo us if we keep on picking ourselves up each time. We shall of course be very muddy and tattered children by the time we reach home. But the bathrooms are all ready, the towels put out, and the clean clothes in the airing cupboard. The only fatal thing is to lose one's temper and give it up. It is when we notice the dirt that God is most present in us: it is the very sign of His presence.[7]

Lewis's encouragement is welcome, isn't it? He writes of "chronic temptations," an apt phrase for the repeating enticements that torment us. Who hasn't battled, again and again, an ingrained weakness or humiliating habit that won't be vanquished? Haven't we, too, had to pick ourselves up, oh, so often, muddy and tattered and grateful for—but almost afraid to return to—home? Who hasn't prayed, "Create in me a *clean* heart, O God"(Psalm 51:10, *King James Version*), while wondering whether God would finally, this time, give up and say, "No, you've fallen once too often, you've tried my endurance for the last time"? Yet He is still Father, and He recognizes our vulnerability, even when we most loudly vaunt our independence.

Marilyn Monroe, who continues to captivate the popular press since her death, has been revealed as much more fragile than her public image hinted during the days of her celebrity. Arthur Miller, one of her former husbands, gives an especially poignant account of her psychic defenselessness in his auto-biography. He quotes Hedda Rosten, a psychiatric social worker who despaired of Marilyn's being able to heal her psychic wounds while working at films. "She is constantly having to test what she hasn't been able to put together yet."[8] She needed relief from the pressure. Her fragile psyche required time and peace for reflection. But, most of all, I'm convinced she needed to find out that she was not merely Marilyn Monroe, sex goddess, but she was Norma Jean, a real person, an individual for whom Christ died, a child whom God loves, a delicate soul too vulnerable to trust herself to the media wolves who wanted only to exploit for their own devilish purposes. In the end, she took her life because she was convinced she had no "home" to return to, no loving parent who wanted only her best, who would take her life into his hands for her own good.

She had not made her "calling and election sure," something 2 Peter 1:10 exhorts Christians to do because, "if you do these things, you will never fall." Our hope is not in our ability to overcome any temptation, something this writer at least has proved unable to do, but is in our relationship with the Father who picks us up and is strong for us. Here's how the apostle Paul puts it: "So, if you think you are standing firm, be careful that you don't fall! No temptation has seized you except what is common to man. And God is faithful; he will not let you be tempted beyond what you can bear. But when you are tempted, he will also provide a way out so that you can stand up under it" (1 Corinthians 10:12, 13).

God's promise is certain. But He isn't to be trifled with. Foolish is the person who deliberately flirts with temptation, either because he feels himself above succumbing or because he believes God will rescue him no matter what. Will Rogers used to talk about a druggist who was asked if he ever took time off to have a good time. The druggist said, no, he didn't, but he sold a lot of headache medicine to those who did.[9] Some people treat God as little more than a morning-after medication who'll undo the damage of the night before, or like a foolish parent who smiles indulgently on the child's self-destructive behavior. God is presented in Scripture as a loving, not a doting, parent. There's a difference. To count on His indulgence "no matter what" is to court disaster.

In a famous passage the great church father Augustine describes how quickly flirting with temptation can do permanent damage to a person's character. A friend of his went under protest to the greatest of Roman festivals, the gladiatorial contests in which human lives were brutally slaughtered while blood-thirsty crowds roared their approval. The young man closed his eyes in order not to see the gladiators butchering one another, the swords flashing, the blood spouting, the wounded falling, victors parading in triumph. But when he heard the yell of excitement from the crowd he opened his eyes, and in a moment he was captured, enjoying the blood and savagery, hollering with delight at the next murder.[10] He hadn't meant to relish the barbarity. He thought he was strong enough to withstand its enchantment. He was wrong.

The stronger you feel, the graver your danger

We seem to be most vulnerable at the point of our greatest strength, undoubtedly because we leave that point unguarded. We don't seek the Lord's help in that area of our lives. We can take care of these matters ourselves. Sometimes we even court disaster by keeping the temptation around— then praying for the Lord to help us resist.

Jay Carty calls this strategy keeping "eclairs in the refrigerator."

> Let's assume you're on a diet, but on the way home you walk by your favorite bakery. The pangs of hunger are overwhelming and at that moment you would rather be fat than hungry, so you go in and

buy two chocolate eclairs. Upon arriving home you're feeling guilty and somewhat defeated so you put the eclairs in the refrigerator and go into the living room where you kneel and pray, "Oh God, help me not to eat those chocolate eclairs."

The hypocrisy in the prayer is palpable. If you really didn't want to eat those eclairs, you wouldn't keep them in the refrigerator, readily available the moment your lust for them overpowers your hatred of your fat! How much power can there be in your prayer?

> You wanted to make sure the pastries wouldn't spoil until you could justify eating them. In other words, *you had already made up your mind to live against your prayers.*[11]

You have merely duped yourself.

Remember 1 Corinthians 10:12? "If you think you are standing firm, be careful that you don't fall!" Gordon MacDonald, onetime president of InterVarsity Christian Fellowship, has shared the story of his unfaithfulness to his wife (and his subsequent repentance and restoration) with his fellow ministers all over the country. He wants to help his colleagues learn from his mistakes. "An unguarded strength and an unprepared heart are double weaknesses," he teaches. He painfully remembers giving a speech at a college commencement. Before the festivities began, a member of that school's board sat with him in the president's office exchanging small talk. MacDonald was asked a question he would later recall with chagrin. "If Satan were to blow you out of the water, how do you think he would do it?"

Gordon didn't know, he told him, but he was certain there was one area in which he wouldn't—his personal relationships. "That's one place I have no doubt that I'm as strong as you can get." He was probably telling the truth. He was happily married to the ideal companion for him. Their relationship was secure. He loved and was loved by his children. His family mattered more to him than anything else in the world except his relationship with God. In that area of his life, he felt invulnerable.

And that's where his world broke open. Only God's grace and his wife's saved his marriage.[12]

John Irving studies temptation with a novelist's irony in his book, *A Prayer for Owen Meany*. Irving depicts Buzzy Thurston, Owen Meany's friend at Gravesend Academy, as an unforgettable illustration of weakness in strength. He embodies all the contradicting idealism and fears of the Vietnam years. There was a lot that Buzzy didn't know, but one thing he knew for sure: he didn't want to go to Nam. After using up his student draft deferment for five years of sports at the state university, Buzzy devised a plan to ensure his ineligibility for the draft. He pumped himself full of poison.

> He drank a fifth of bourbon a day for two weeks; he smoked so much marijuana that his hair smelled like a cupboard crammed with oregano; he started a fire in his parents' oven, baking peyote; he was hospitalized with a colon disorder, following an LSD experience wherein he became convinced that his own Hawaiian sports shirt was edible, and he consumed some of it—including the buttons and the contents of the pocket: a book of matches, a package of cigarette papers, and a paper clip.

It worked. The Gravesend draft board declared Buzzy "psychologically unfit to serve," which had been "his crafty intention." It worked too well. Along the way he had grown to *like* the bourbon, the peyote, and the LSD. He was killed one night on the Maiden Hill Road by the steering column of his Plymouth when he drove head-on into the abutment of the railroad bridge. His excesses killed him.[13] The drugs he was using used him. He fooled the draft board. And himself.

Readers of this book are not going to find the drugs that killed Buzzy much of a temptation. You and I fight a different temptation. We want to be religiously strong. We pray, read our Bibles, attend our studies, sit on our committees, memorize our verses, sanitize our speech, guard against associating with the wrong people, pay attention to all things great and small that characterize the spiritually muscular. We thank God that we are not like other people.

Then along comes Richard Foster to warn the religiously rigorous that we are in grave danger. Cautioning that "power can be an extremely destructive thing in any context," Foster contends the employment of power "in the service of religion . . . is downright diabolical." Religious power is destructive in a way that no other type of power is. Quoting Lord Asquith's famous axiom that power corrupts and absolute power corrupts absolutely, he applies it to religion. It's altogether too easy for religious people to convince ourselves we are above normal law; beneath our mantle of piety we feel incorruptible, which makes us especially so. "When we are convinced that what we are doing is identical with the kingdom of God, anyone who opposes us *must* be wrong. When we are convinced that we always use our power to good ends, we believe we can never do wrong."[14]

In recent years we've seen the fall of enough television evangelists and other religious leaders to need no more proof that Foster is right. Paul said, "When I am weak, then I am strong" (2 Corinthians 12:10). The converse is also true: "When I am ([or feel I am) strong, then I am weak."

Help is always at hand

How are we to resist, then, the temptations that bedevil us? It's helpful to remember our heritage as God's vulnerable, none-too-strong children, but what then? Remembering isn't enough. Resisting is essential. But if we aren't strong enough to resist the devil's lures on our own, then how do we do it? These practical steps will help:

1) **"Fix [y]our eyes *on* Jesus"** as Hebrews 12:2 recommends. He's the best example we can find. He overcame. So can we, to the extent we become like Him.

2) **Be open to receive help *from* Jesus.** Hebrews 4:14-16 calls Him our "great high priest" who is able "to sympathize with our weaknesses" because He "has been tempted in every way, just as we are—yet was without sin." Thanks to Him, we can "approach the throne of grace with confidence, so that we may receive mercy and find grace to help us in our time of need."

3) **Get your help from the same place Jesus got His—God's Word.** Matthew 4:1-11 tells the story of Jesus' severe testing in the wilderness at the beginning of His ministry. As

has often been pointed out, the devil tempted Jesus at the point of His strength. He was embarking on His God-commissioned service to mankind. He was filled with desire to do His Father's will. The devil slyly offered Him some shortcuts.

In God's name He would feed the hungry—including himself. *". . . tell these stones to become bread."*

The people would question His credentials. But if they knew He had jumped from the highest point of the temple and walked away unscathed, no one would doubt who He was. *". . . throw yourself down."*

His authority would be challenged by high officials who would do everything in their power to abort His mission. If only they knew of His political clout, they'd get out of His way. *"All this [the kingdoms of the world and their splendor] I will give you if you will bow down and worship me."*

As Philip Yancey correctly observes, "All three of the 'temptations' lay within Jesus' grasp; all three were, in fact, His prerogatives."[15] The devil wasn't offering anything more than what Jesus deserved. Yet He resisted the temptations, in each instance buttressing himself with Scripture:

Bread? *"Man does not live on bread alone, but on every word that comes from the mouth of God."*

Celebrity, proof of identity? *"Do not put the Lord your God to the test."*

Political clout? *"Worship the Lord your God, and serve him only."*

Malcolm Muggeridge suggests in his *Christ and the Media* that if Jesus were going through the wilderness temptation today, there would be a fourth temptation: to appear on national television![16]

What impresses Matthew's readers is Jesus' preparation for His ministry. He has been getting ready for a lifetime—in His parents' godly home, in the synagogue, in His study of Scripture, with His keen eye for the working of God in everyday experiences among people of every walk of life. But still He makes His first move after His baptism a spiritual retreat in the wilderness, another kind of baptism (one we would call a "baptism by fire") in which He wrestles with His destiny, His chief adversary planting these disturbing thoughts, wafting Him aloft to temple pinnacle or mountain's peak. He has a job to do; will He do it God's way or the devil's? How to be sure which is which? What exactly is it He is to do for His Father? And what's the most appropriate method? How can He know?

We have read to the end of the story, so we know how Jesus makes His way through this wilderness and through the even more severe tests to come. He passes every one, including the ones in Gethsemane and on Golgotha. He finishes well because He begins well, here in the wilderness, wrestling with His chief adversary, besting him with the Word of the Lord.

He does not forget who He is.

Nor do we.

How can a young man keep his way pure?
By living according to your word. . . .
I have hidden your word in my heart
that I might not sin against you (Psalm 119:9, 11).

Chapter 11

When You Can't Trust Anybody

Micah 7:1-10

The prophet Micah preached in Samaria and in Jerusalem during the last quarter of the eighth century before Christ. Like our own, Micah's era was one of extremes, great wealth on the one hand, dreadful poverty on the other. Everywhere he looked the prophet encountered corruption and dishonesty. Every man was out for himself. The courts of justice and the tents of the priesthood were not exempt. Where could Micah find anybody he could trust?

Utter discouragement, v. 1

You already know where I'm going, don't you? Read our newspapers, watch our television programs, listen to the radio and you come to the same disheartening conclusion about our era. Can you trust anybody? Can you trust this author? It's one thing for a preacher to wax optimistic as he trumpets *victory in Jesus*. It's quite another thing to be forced to deal daily with priests and judges and businessmen and people in the trades who are on the take. Fighting for survival among the predators is hardly anyone's idea of victorious living.

Very early in our marriage Joy and I realized we couldn't trust everybody (not a happy awakening for the couple of *naïfs* we were at the time). How were we to deal with people who wouldn't deal honestly? We didn't feel comfortable operating on their standard (besides, we weren't good at it), so we adopted a slogan we've kept ever since: "We'd rather get taken than take." We had already learned the hard way that we couldn't always tell the crook from the legitimate seller. Purchasing a certain car before we were married was a big lesson for me. We paid for my mistake for longer than I like to admit. That lesson was the first of many.

As recently as the month following our son's death we dealt with a vulture. Lane had entered into an agreement with a woman who, it appeared to us, was robbing his limited estate of any remaining value. We had enough informants and witnesses against her that we probably could have taken her to court. Once again, though, we found ourselves quoting our old slogan. We were getting taken but we didn't fight back. Winning a court case wouldn't bring our son back, and compared with losing him, nothing else seemed very important.

So what do *you* do when it seems you can't trust anybody?

A prophet of God isn't needed to convince us there's corruption in this world and that when you are trying to live a Christian life, you may very well be cheated because you can't do unto others what they're getting away with doing unto you. But who hasn't felt like wailing with Micah, "What misery is mine!"

Are the words Micah's or God's? In chapter six, God has been speaking through the prophet. Is He still in the seventh? Or is this Micah's voice? It doesn't matter. On this subject, Micah and God see things alike:

> What misery is mine!
> I am like one who gathers summer fruit
> at the gleaning of the vineyard [*at the end of the harvest when everything has been pretty much picked over and just a few leavings remain*];
> There is no cluster of grapes to eat,
> none of the early figs that I crave.

I get only the leftovers! Reason enough to be discouraged. Shattered expectations. Who hasn't prayed and prayed earnestly, "O God, please do this for me," and He doesn't. Or "God, please look after my family, I am placing them in Your care," and it appears He has neglected them. Or "God, don't let this tragedy happen," and it happens anyway. You become utterly discouraged. Can't you trust anybody, even God? Where is somebody who cares?

I spoke for a breakfast meeting at a recent national convention of persons involved in urban ministries. The program committee asked me to talk about the church in the inner city. I welcomed the opportunity to tell them how much I admire the work they do, often in the most difficult circumstances. I believe that in the city—and I mean in downtown urban areas, in the blackened heart of the metropolis—is where the church ought to be. The body of Christ is wanted there because it is the one organization that exists strictly for the sake of the people there. It has no ulterior motive. It exists to serve. Period.

What is true of people in the inner city is true of people everywhere: everybody needs a community of persons who are "there" for them, who serve without seeking profit or glory but simply the satisfaction inherent in serving and saving people who would otherwise be lost. You and I and everyone else need persons to whom we can turn in trust. There are plenty of the other kind.

Human depravity, vv. 2-4

The godly have been swept from the land;
not one upright man remains.

Micah is exaggerating. Like most of us preachers, he employs a little hyperbole in the service of the truth. It isn't literally true there's not an upright person left, but it is true that's how it feels when it seems everybody is taking advantage of you.

All men lie in wait to shed blood [*some people would rather fight than switch, than do almost anything*];
each hunts his brother with a net.

> Both hands are skilled in doing evil *[they are ambidextrously
> evil];*
> the ruler *[who is charged with the duty of bringing peace and
> order to his society]* demands gifts,
> the judge accepts bribes.

No justice. Money talks, and talks corruptly.

When the O. J. Simpson trial dominated the headlines, several questions nagged. Is it possible for O. J. to get a fair trial? Won't he receive prejudicial treatment because he's a wealthy celebrity? He can afford the most expensive attorneys. His money can manipulate the media. Will it be possible to find unbiased jurors? Such questions were asked by people who believed there was no way he would be declared guilty, because of his celebrity status. What if O. J. had been a typical African-American male, they wondered. What then?

The distrust had less to do with the famous football star than with America's criminal justice system. Was it possible for truth and justice to prevail in a judiciary system so tainted by money?

> The judge accepts bribes,
> the powerful dictate what they desire—
> they all conspire together.

Micah captures a familiar feeling of helplessness here, the hopelessness of everybody except the wealthy or politically powerful when going up against "the system."

> The best of them is like a brier,
> the most upright worse than a thorn hedge.

Because things are so bad, the preacher warns:

> The day of your watchmen has come *[he's talking to the
> evildoers],*
> the day God visits you.

But for the evildoers' victims, there's hope. Micah's tone changes:

> Now is the time of *their* [the corrupt ones'] confusion.

Micah has dramatically captured the despondence of the disenfranchised, the sense of futility that overwhelms the petitioner at city hall (at the door of almost any government bureau) or the poor anywhere. What can you do when you're broke, when your back is against the wall and it feels like everybody is against you? Is nobody to be trusted?

What would Micah have made of a group of American young people on a goodwill tour to Japan a few years ago? Members of a marching band from Texas Southern University in Houston traveled to Japan to enhance relations between our two countries. When it came time for the students to return however, they were not allowed to leave Japan until the police could recover all the things the goodwill ambassadors had shoplifted. Their goodwill tour had turned into a shoplifting spree. They filched twenty-two thousand dollars worth of goods from department stores, including more than eighty CD players, miniature TVs, pocket recorders, electric razors, and the like. Police kept the buses from leaving for the airport until the loot had been returned. American students, in Japan to make friends of the Japanese, ripped them off instead.[1]

If you can't trust goodwill ambassadors, then whom?

Charles Colson, reflecting on the 1980s, borrowed a phrase Aleksandr Solzhenitsyn's used in his 1978 Harvard address to describe our society. The Russian author referred to ours as a "morally exhausted" society. To underscore his insight, Colson ticked off the following list:

- Ivan Boesky and his sort, imprisoned for using insider information to bilk billions from unsuspecting victims
- Public officials skimming millions from HUD programs for the poor
- Military officers trading honor for money or sex
- Savings and loan companies being looted for 150 billion dollars
- Scores of politicians being caught in scandals of sex or greed
- Religious hucksters carving out their personal fiefdoms
- Government tripling the national debt from one to three trillion dollars.

The common thread running through all? "The notion that life somehow gives us the right to have every whim and desire satisfied." It is, says Colson, "a looter's ethic."[2]

In a society ruled by the looter's ethic, you quickly infer you can't trust anybody, especially your governors. A midwest university president discovered this mistrust in, of all places, an adult Sunday school class he was teaching in the fall of 1987. Comprised of the community's bankers, executives, university professors, the group was discussing the Iran-Contra scandal, which was just then unfolding. Americans had heard that in the Persian Gulf an Iranian ship had been sunk. Iran claimed an American ship had torpedoed it. The American government protested that the ship had exploded upon hitting an Iranian mine. The teacher asked his class a straightforward question: Do you believe Iran's story or the American government's? To the last person in the room, they asked for more facts before they would make a decision. Not a single person trusted their administration to tell the truth.[3]

How long do you think a democratic nation will survive when the people cannot trust their leaders? An old Masai marriage proverb applies here: "The neck cannot go above the head."

Natural reaction, vv. 5, 6

If you can't trust your leaders, what will you do? In such a society, the natural reaction is exactly what Micah describes in verses 5 and 6.

> Do not trust a neighbor;
>   put no confidence in a friend.
> Even with her who lies in your embrace
>   be careful of your words

How would you like to live like this?

> For a son dishonors his father,
>   a daughter rises up against her mother,
> a daughter-in-law against her mother-in-law—
>   a man's enemies are the members of his own household.

Where do you turn when you can't even trust your family? What could be scarier than to dwell with enemies in your own household?

In the ninth grade I was given one of the leads in our high school's production of *Pinocchio*. The director made it very clear that I was chosen, not for any talent, but because I had a big nose. Poor Pinocchio—every time he told a lie his nose would grow. Don't you wish everybody's did? What a help that would be in business transactions, in family disputes, in all human activities. Honesty would be the norm, and truth would prevail.

Now the opposite is true. Technology has made it possible to alter photographs and soundtracks so that the layperson can't tell the difference between a truthful representation and a doctored one. You can't trust recorded evidence. More than ever we need to resurrect the Old Testament law: "You shall not give false testimony." The law prohibits false testimony to protect the truth.

In the New Testament Paul words the prohibition more bluntly in Ephesians 4:25: "Each of you must put off falsehood and speak truthfully to his neighbor, for we are all members of one body." His injunction adds the motive: we belong to each other. But surely Paul's directive is unnecessary. Would members of the same body lie to each other? Yes. Like their descendants of every generation, the saints in Ephesus found it much too easy to slip into lying for self-preservation or profit. Being completely honest was as difficult for them as for us. One of the reasons we suspect other people of dishonesty is that we employ it so well.

In his commentary on *Deuteronomy*, Jewish author Mordecai Richler recalls his childhood when, after school one day, he had slipped into Kresge's store and shoplifted. The Scots Presbyterian manager nabbed him. He wasn't angry, he said, but ashamed for Richler's sake. "I never would have expected such behavior from a Jewish lad. You come from such a hard-working and law-abiding people—a people I greatly admire because you have always put education, sobriety, and family above all."

Yes, Richler admitted, that was his people's reputation, but how did they get it? He considers his ancestors in Moab:

> a loutish lot, a bunch of good ol' boys, much given to carousing, wenching, pilfering, fighting, and sacking cities. Who knew them better than Moses? His time short, he warns his flock that they will be cursed if they lead blind men astray, remove neighbor's land-

marks, take advantage of widows and orphans, accept pay to murder an innocent person, or lie with their father's wife, or sisters, or beasts.[4]

As Richler makes clear, Moses' greatness lay in his super-human attempt to bring order to anarchy, civility to men who "lie in wait to shed blood." He knew "the best of them is like a brier, the most upright worse than a thorn hedge." They were an uninstructed, unconverted, undisciplined people whose future was destruction—except for Moses. He would literally "lay down the law" to them. To the extent they heeded his domesticating word, they could flourish. They were surrounded by enemies. They had to learn to trust one another—and be trustworthy enough to be trusted—or they would perish. The Law would be their guide.

In a much more recent era, Alan Redpath, a leader in the Church of England, visited his friends the Ted Engstroms in Nairobi, Kenya. In honor of his visit, a number of the Kenyan leaders came for a meal with him. As they were eating, they began to give him their perspective on the missionary activities in their country. It was all negative. In frustration and grief, Redpath asked, "Did we do nothing right?"

After a pause, one of them spoke up, "Yes, yes. You did do something right. You gave us the standard by which to judge you. If you had not shown us the truth of Christ you would not have put yourself so badly in the dark."[5]

Cause of the despondency, v. 9

The African's response introduces one of the roles of the church in this confused age. The church has the responsibility for speaking the truth, especially when it's unpopular. The Christian's duty is to speak and to live the truth, even when it's not welcome.

Did you notice verse 9? Micah speaks here as the nation of Israel:

> Because I have sinned against him,
> I will bear the Lord's wrath until he pleads my case and establishes my right.

"Because *I* have sinned." This is the bottom line. Micah identifies himself with his people. A basic tenet we learned in elementary psychology class is that we tend to project on to other people our own problems and sins. Whenever you hear someone say, "You just can't trust anybody," guard your assets. He understands deception all too well.

His experience hasn't been mine, though. It probably hasn't been yours, either. There are trustworthy people out there. Listen to them carefully. Like Micah, they are acutely aware of their own propensity to sin. They admit it. They do not close their eyes to the corruption around them, but neither do they boast of their superiority to it. They know that they who live in the midst of a people of unclean lips have trouble keeping their own clean. They look above them for the sinlessness they don't find in themselves.

Gail Sheehy's biography of Mikhail Gorbachev describes the Russian leader as a person of very high intelligence and energy, a man who really did want to bring about change in the Soviet Russia but who, because he had lived so long within that corrupt system, had himself become deformed by it. He was aware of its depravity; he even quarreled with it, but he tolerated a great deal in it in order to escape a fate in the Gulag. His toleration of Brezhnev's system warped him.

You and I live in a corrupt system as well and no doubt have been deformed by it in ways we are unaware of. But we are not left without hope.

Trust in God, vv. 7-10

At the beginning of this chapter I told you of our being cheated by one grasping person when we were taking care of our son Lane's effects. What I didn't tell you then is that we were treated graciously, respectfully, and honestly by several others who, if they had wanted, were also in a position to gain something for themselves at our expense, but they didn't do so. They proved trustworthy.

This chapter's title, "When You Can't Trust Anybody," is misleading. I have never been in a position where I couldn't trust anybody. That's in part because all my life I've hung around Christians. I don't mean there are no dishonest

Christians; there are. Hypocrisy is to be found everywhere, even in church. But I do mean that there are genuinely honest Christians whom you can trust with your life, your possessions, with everything. I must also admit, by the way, I've been blessed by some very honest non-Christians too; we don't hold the corner on integrity.

> Because I have sinned against him *[God]*,
> I will bear the Lord's wrath.

Micah will bear that burden of his sin, he will experience what it is to be at odds with God. His whole lament is that of a person who, because he has sinned against God is out of sorts with the world. His source of despondency is himself, not God, not the world.

Recently a member of our church asked me, in light of Lane's death, "How can you keep going? Don't you have doubts?" A good question, one I've tried to answer as candidly as possible. Yes, I have some really big questions I'm going to ask God some day.

How do I keep going? Joy and I trust in God. We can't answer all the haunting questions but at this stage of our lives, we've walked with the Lord a long time and we've been, as some people say, "down on our luck" more than once. But what has kept us going has been His trustworthiness and, we would have to add, the trustworthiness of His people who have walked with us. We have found in Him and in them sources of strength without which we wouldn't know how to keep going.

That's why, in dealing with this Scripture, we can bear Micah's complaint. We know that the words will turn, as Micah's do, to the light. Look at the seventh verse:

> But as for me . . . .

Underscore that simple phrase. Micah's society and ours are corrupt, full of every kind of evil, but we don't have to buy into the corruption.

> *But as for me,* I watch in hope for the Lord,
> I wait for God my Savior; my God will hear me.

Before the ringing affirmation with which the sentence ends, the introductory clause makes way for it. When you are discouraged and it looks as if everything is going against you, when people are lying and cheating, you have a choice to make: Will you become one of them or not? Will you give in? You will unless you have previously said, "But as for me . . . ." And then, having succumbed to their immorality you will give in to their despondency. When it appears you can't trust anybody you must resolve to be the one person who can be trusted. In your victory over cheapened behavior lies your victory over discouragement. You have decided: if they lie to you, you will not lie in return. If they cheat you, they will never be cheated by you. If they take your money, they will never rob you of your character.

Micah's "but as for me" evokes a wonderful passage at the end of the book of Joshua (24:14, 15). The fading leader challenges the children of Israel to be faithful to God even after Joshua will no longer be with them. They are ready to claim the promised land. Joshua urges them to "fear the Lord and serve him with all faithfulness." They had worshiped others gods in Egypt. "Throw away the gods your forefathers worshiped beyond the River and in Egypt," he tells them, "and serve the Lord." If they prefer to keep their old gods, they may. He won't force them to serve God against their will. Then he adds:

> But as for me and my household, we will serve the Lord.

There they are again, those indispensable words: "But as for me . . . ."

They are the words of maturity. In the process of growing up, the day comes for every person when the stand must be taken—against the evils of society, against the temptations of the mind, the enticements of the flesh, the so-called justice of "an eye for an eye and a tooth for a tooth." It seems almost impossible to do so unless you can also say with Micah, "I wait for God my Savior; my God will hear me."

That was the seventh verse. Now the eighth:

Do not gloat over me, my enemy!

You may have cheated me out of some money, you may have even defeated me in court. Yes, I have fallen and you are observing my humiliation but:

> Though I have fallen, I will rise.
> Though I sit in darkness *[and seem to be a loser]*,
> the Lord will be my light.

Things won't look good for me for a while. But I don't despair: He will plead my case. Micah's assurance is palpable: "*until* he pleads my case," not *if* He pleads my case.

> He will bring me out into the light;
>   I will see his righteousness.
> Then my enemy will see it
>   and will be covered with shame,
> she who said to me,
>   "Where is the Lord your God?"

The Lord our God has been with us in the darkness and if we'll give Him a chance, He will bring us to the light.

When the Lord is your God, you never feel the need to say, "You just can't trust anybody."

Chapter 12

When Everybody Is Complaining

Numbers 11:1-9, 13-15, 23

Lord, I need to talk to You about a problem, or maybe an opportunity. I feel as if I'm being tested in a very hard way. Lately, I've been praying for a couple of things. One, that You would give me wisdom. I'm learning that You don't give wisdom, that it must be taught through different experiences, and that teaching is not a short term deal. I guess this will just take time. The second area I've prayed about is that You would make an example of me that speaks to people I come in contact with about You and how good You are. I want my faith to be visible in such a way that those I come in contact with can see it and know that You are at work in my life according to how I conduct myself. Maybe what I'm experiencing is a result of these prayers. But, God, I need to understand what's going on, to know that You are in control, and that I'm not alone and going through these times for nothing.

My friend let me eavesdrop on his conversation with God. On his computer he had poured out his frustration. He seemed to have lost any sense of his victory in Jesus. A host of problems had piled up on him, all of which he laid before the Lord. One of his former employees was suing him and one of the expensive products his company sells had been returned, costing several hundred thousand dollars he didn't have. An order for another had just been canceled. His daughter's wedding was coming up and he didn't have any money. He couldn't give her the gift he had promised. He had excessive business expenses and there were other lawsuits beside the big one. The economy had turned sour, forcing him to lay off some valuable employees. He couldn't recall greater stress. He was afraid he was going to lose his business. He had to talk to God about it.

When things are bleak, when it seems that everybody's complaining to you and about you—and you're complaining as well—you do the most natural thing for a believer in God. You take your lamentations to Him.

Complaining begets complaining, vv. 1-9

This was Moses' method, according to Numbers 11. Leading the nation of Israel from captivity in Egypt to freedom in the promised land has been the most difficult challenge of Moses' existence, a forty-year endurance test. God has taken care of them, as He promised. He has provided their daily manna, but they are disgruntled. You can get your fill of manna pretty quickly.

> Now the people complained about their hardships in the hearing of the Lord, and when he heard them his anger was aroused. Then fire from the Lord burned among them and consumed some of the outskirts of the camp. When the people cried out to Moses, he prayed to the Lord and the fire died down. So that place was called Taberah, because fire from the Lord had burned among them.

Moses prays for them and the Lord responds. Still they won't stop their bellyaching. It begins, as it so often does, with "the rabble":

> The rabble with them began to crave other food, and again the Israelites started wailing and said, 'If only we had meat to eat! We remember the fish we ate in Egypt at no cost—also the cucumbers, melons, leeks, onions and garlic.

Sound familiar? "Oh, how well we ate in those days, back in Egypt, before this Moses fellow interfered." They probably aren't exaggerating, either. They had eaten better. What they're not admitting, though, is that they were well-fed *slaves* then, shackled by the Pharaoh's tyranny. The food was better, but what a price they paid for it. Like humanity everywhere, the grumblers were remembering selectively, recalling the food and forgetting the bondage.

> But now we have lost our appetite; we never see anything but this manna!

The manna was like coriander seed and looked like resin. The people went around gathering it, and then ground it in a hand mill or crushed it in a mortar. They cooked it in a pot or made it into cakes, and it tasted like something made with olive oil. When the dew settled on the camp at night, the manna also came down.

So they have, in fact, been fed. God hasn't let them go hungry in the wilderness—but their sensitive palates crave a more refined cuisine:

> Moses heard the people of every family wailing, each at the entrance to his tent.

What started with the rabble now infects every family. Complaining is contagious. You're susceptible, too, aren't you? You've been in conversations with persons who major in dissecting every social ill. Before you know it, you're chiming in, offering your personal examples to prove the critic right. "Oh, you're so right. In fact, just the other day I . . . ." And you're off. You probably weren't even upset about the issue until prompted by the critic, but now you've become infected.

The worst thing about belly-aching is that you hear yourself doing it. Your own words increase your displeasure. What was a mild irritant becomes, as you wax more vehement, an intolerable burden.

The Old Testament records many laments. Whole books are devoted to complaints (*Ecclesiastes* and *Lamentations,* for example). They make for depressing reading. It's especially depressing in the early books of the Bible, in which God is rescuing the nation but the ungrateful people are finding so much fault. God is rescuing them from slavery and granting them liberty, but they experience the transition as too much change (from Egypt to the land of Canaan) and too much sameness (a boring consistency of diet that drives them mad).

They hate the monotony of the manna almost as much as the uncertainty of the transition. Almost, but not quite. What they want most of all is to go back to the way things used to be. They don't like it outside their comfort zone.

As a rule, human beings are conservatives. We prefer the way things were to the way they might be. We resist change in a growing church, for example, where new people dislocate older members who, without even realizing what they are doing, freeze out the newcomers. A major reason most churches remain small is that the charter members like it just the way it always has been. They prefer stagnation to the tensions of change.

Complaining sometimes seems justified, vv. 10-15

Tension is exactly what the children of Israel are feeling, so Moses sends up a complaint of his own:

> Why have you brought this trouble on your servant? What have I done to displease you that you put the burden of all these people on me?

Moses is uttering every leader's prayer. More than once in my life I have prayed, "Lord, what did I do wrong that You gave me this church, or these leaders, or this dilemma?" At the time, people were complaining to and about me as the Israelites were complaining to and about Moses. Where can the leader turn at such a time, if not to the One who called him to leadership in the first place? Thus Moses:

> What have I done to displease you that you put the burden of all these people on me? Did I conceive all these people? Did I give them birth? *[Are they my troublesome kids?]* Why do you tell me to carry them in my arms, as a nurse carries an infant, to the land you promised on oath to their forefathers?"

His prayer turns from a general complaint to the specific problem:

Where can I get meat for all these people? They keep wailing to me, "Give us meat to eat!"

The problem is symptomatic, however, of the interminable details Moses must tend to. He's tired:

I cannot carry all these people by myself; the burden is too heavy for me.

You can see, can't you, how this Scripture fits in a book on victorious living? Who hasn't been in Moses' shoes, struggling to solve problems beyond your ability, sinking under a load of responsibility far greater than you have the ability or resources to carry? You feel anything but victorious. You're prayers don't burst with enthusiasm. They sound just like Moses', "This burden is too heavy for me."

If this is how you are going to treat me, put me to death right now—if I have found favor in your eyes—and do not let me face my own ruin.

This prayer does violence to our usual image of Moses. The words sound suicidal. He's had it. Things are about as bad as they can be. He wants out.

A recent cartoon depicts two desperate men crawling across the hot, barren desert. They look up to see a camel coming toward them, but the camel is also crawling. "Well," one grumbles to the other, "this isn't a cheerful sight."

As far as Moses is concerned, the sight of his teeming tribes angrily whining about their provisions isn't cheerful, either. His shoulders sag under the burden of leadership. The movement of his prayer is downward:

The Lord caused this trouble (v. 10).
I must have displeased Him (v. 11).
Are these people my responsibility (v. 12)?
Why me (v. 12)?
How can I make them happy (v. 13)?
The load is too much for me (v. 14)!
I want to die (v. 15).

If there are Christian leaders anywhere who haven't complained like Moses against the tribulations of leadership, I haven't met them. The ones I know could identify with him—and with the pastor of Lover's Lane United Methodist Church in Dallas. After leading his congregation in constructing a new building on a sixteen-acre plot, he was visited by a friend who was puzzled by what seemed to be the inappropriate location of his study. The building sat at the edge of the property along a busy four-lane highway, and the pastor's study was at the end of the building, right beside that highway. The friend studied the noisy traffic outside the window. "Tom," he asked, "why in the world with all these sixteen acres of land to build on, did you put your study here by that infernal traffic?!" Tom looked out the window awhile, then answered wistfully, "Sometimes I just like to stand here and watch something moving that I didn't have to push."[1]

Moses would have understood. He'd been pushing—and pulling—hard. His efforts were not appreciated.

The discouraged leader could have written Psalm 77, one of many hymns of complaint in the Psalms. Listen, though, for the seed of hope it contains.

> I cried out to God for help;
>   I cried out to God to hear me.
> When I was in distress, I sought the Lord;
>   at night I stretched out untiring hands
>   and my soul refused to be comforted.

As I said, we've been there. We understand. But listen to that last line again:

> And my soul refused to be comforted.

Could this be a source of our misery? Is it possible our distress is magnified by our refusal to hear, to believe, to trust the Lord, to accept with thanksgiving the help He offers? Were you brought up like me to be self-sufficient, independent? Did your parents encourage you to think, to do, to manage for yourself? ("Come over here," my Dad would tell me when I had fallen down, "and I'll help you up.") Did your parents so strongly stress your need to be responsible that even today, when you are in trouble (whether of your own making or another's) you believe you must assume full responsibility and expect no help from anyone else? And then do you complain because you just can't do so much by yourself? Do you wonder where God is when you need Him most? Or do you pray, "Lord help me," but not count on any assistance from His direction? ("Come over here," you think God is telling you, "and after you've picked yourself up to get over here, I'll help you.")

Our daughter Kim was only three years old when she gave her mother and me an unforgettable lesson in self-sufficiency that goes too far. She was working with her mother in the kitchen and Joy, watching her ineffectively stirring the dough, offered to help her. Kim would have none of it. "I'd rather do it my selfish," she insisted.

Wouldn't we all? Kim's word was the right one. We want to be in charge, to prove we can be responsible, to do things our own way. Nothing wrong—unless by so insisting we botch the job. Then to persist in error is, well, it's selfish. And our souls refuse to be comforted:

> I remembered you, O God, and I groaned;
> I mused, and my spirit grew faint.

Thinking about God doesn't bring the psalmist relief. He is more discouraged than before.

> You kept my eyes from closing *[I'm losing sleep now because God won't let me sleep! Somehow it's His fault.]*;
> I was too troubled to speak.
> I thought about the former days,
>   the years of long ago;
> I remembered my songs in the night.
>   My heart mused and my spirit inquired:
> "Will the Lord reject forever?
>   Will he never show his favor again?
> Has his unfailing love vanished forever?
>   Has his promise failed for all time?
> Has God forgotten to be merciful?
>   Has he in anger withheld his compassion?"
> Then I thought, "To this I will appeal:

the years of the right hand of the Most High."
I will remember the deeds of the Lord;
yes, I will remember your miracles of long ago.
I will meditate on all your works
and consider all your mighty deeds.
Your ways, O God, are holy.
What god is so great as our God?
You are the God who performs miracles;
you display your power among the peoples.

His song goes on, but this is enough for our purposes. His *remembering* what God has done overcomes his discouragement.

When you are caught in the throes of self-pity, when you think nobody has had it as bad as you've had it, remember the good times, the closeness, the blessings. Life hasn't been all bad. Remember your friends, also, your loved ones who have walked with you through the valley of the shadow of death. Remember and give thanks. Your attitude will improve, even if your immediate situation does not.

The Lord hears and answers, vv. 16-22

Let's return to Numbers 11 now. As the psalmist turns to the Lord in grateful remembering, so Moses turns to God in his desperation, and the Lord hears and answers. We begin with verse 16:

> The Lord said to Moses: "Bring me seventy of Israel's elders who are known to you as leaders and officials among the people. Have them come to the Tent of Meeting, that they may stand there with you. I will come down and speak with you there, and I will take of the Spirit that is on you and put the Spirit on them. They will help you carry the burden of the people so that you will not have to carry it alone.
> "Tell the people: 'Consecrate yourselves in preparation for tomorrow, when you will eat meat. The Lord heard you when you wailed, "If only we had meat to eat! We were better off in Egypt!" Now the Lord will give you meat, and you will eat it.'"

We stop here to consider the kind of help God sends. We often overemphasize our walk with the Lord and underemphasize our fellowship with our companions along the way. The New Testament instructs us to "carry each other's burdens, and in this way you will fulfill the law of Christ" (Galatians 6:2). It is not God's desire that we take on life single-handedly. When times are good we may think we can do it. We feel strong, self-sufficient. But when trouble strikes, we discover our deficiencies. God's solution to Moses' desperation is not different from what He has provided for us in the church, where we bear each other's burdens and bolster one another as we walk through the valleys of death, desperation, and heartache.

One of the Lawsons' great blessings is in never having felt isolated or abandoned in our ministry in Mesa. We have an outstanding staff, supportive eldership, and rich fellowship among the members. Their partnership has propped us up through the years. The outpouring of love and prayers we received when our son died surpassed anything we had ever experienced. We were at the low point of our lives. We had used all the spiritual and emotional resources at our command to get through the distress of those awful days. We had nothing to give in return. Our loved ones knew it and reached out to us in ways we couldn't have anticipated. Unable to carry the load ourselves, we were carried along until we returned to life.

Our experience then explains why this passage speaks so clearly to me now. Moses was in his own pit of depression, and God urged him to let his people come to his rescue. The Lord used seventy carefully selected men to sustain him. "You don't have to do this all alone, Moses; here are seventy others—share the load with them. I'll put my Spirit in them as I put my Spirit in you. They'll be competent; you can trust them. I don't expect you to carry this load by yourself."

While I was in the midst of my study of this Scripture, Scott Monfort, one of our church leaders, gave me a delightful present. A member of the Air National Guard, Scott made special arrangements for me to fly in a KC135, a fuel tanker. With a handful of others I boarded the big flying service station. Our assignment was to fuel a couple of F16s mid-flight. Our route took us over parts of Arizona, New Mexico, and Utah. I lay face down in the boom bay at about 23,000 feet watching as the fighter planes pulled up just behind and below the KC135. The boom operator expertly lowered the hose into the fuel tanks. Filling gasoline tanks was one of my jobs in my parents' service station and grocery store, but I never in my wildest dreams thought of refueling a plane flying three or four hundred miles an hour. It was an exciting day.

As I said, I was studying this passage that week, just a little over a month after Lane died. The parallel was too obvious to ignore.

Those F16s are fine, fast, fighter planes but they can't fly great distances without refueling; they burn the aviation fuel too fast. Their tank capacity is too small. They can do their jobs only by pulling up to a larger, fuller, stronger plane, to gain renewed strength to go on.

That is what Joy and I had been doing in those weeks when our reserves were depleted. We sought the Lord and He heard. We relaxed into the strength of the church. What we could not do, others did for us. They wrote, they prayed, they hugged, they cried, they worked—and their strength renewed our own.

May I mention parenthetically the value of belonging not only to a church, but more specifically to a small congregation within a church (if yours like ours is a large one)? I do my best to convince our members that they must, for their own sakes, belong to a small group, a Sunday school class, Family Circle (our home Bible studies), or some other band of mutually-supportive persons, in which they know the members and are known by them, so that if they are absent they're missed, and if others are not present they miss and check up on them.

While I was typing this page a friend telephoned. He had had a very bad weekend. His adult son had tried to commit suicide. We were grateful that his attempt had failed, but my friend and his wife had been through ten harrowing days of not knowing where their son was nor what condition he was in. He called me because he knew I would understand and, though I couldn't do anything physical for him, having a friend who knew and who cared was enough. Had the father and I not been longtime fellow workers in the kingdom, I wouldn't have known and couldn't have been there for him—as, I should add, he was there for me when I called to tell him of our son's successful attempt.

The genius of the Christian walk is that we invest our lives in one another so that when the need arises, we have earned the right to be of help.

Help is what the Lord wanted Moses to have, so He called for the seventy men. Then He gave the people what they wanted. They wanted meat, they got meat!

> Now the Lord will give you meat, and you will eat it. You will not eat it for just one day, or two days, or five, ten or twenty days, but for a whole month—until it comes out of your nostrils and you loathe it—because you have rejected the Lord, who is among you, and have wailed before him, saying, "Why did we ever leave Egypt?"

But Moses still hasn't fully caught on. He challenges God again in verse 21:

> Here I am among six hundred thousand men on foot, and you say, "I will give them meat to eat for a whole month!"

He remains under the illusion that he has to find the food by himself. He can't forget he's the leader, responsible for this host. Would they have enough if flocks and herds were slaughtered for them? Would they have enough if all the fish in the sea were caught for them?

"What am I going to do, Lord?"

The moral of the story

God's answer to Moses is one every praying believer has heard:

> Is the Lord's arm too short?

"Come on, Moses, you're dealing with God here. I don't expect you to do it all, that's my job. You just trust me and they'll be fed."

The rest of the story is simply told. They are fed. Boy, are they fed.

> Now a wind went out from the Lord and drove quail in from the sea. It brought them down all around the camp to about three feet above the ground, as far as a day's walk in any direction. All that day and night and all the next day the people went out and gathered quail. No one gathered less than ten homers. Then they spread them out all around the camp.

You have to be careful how you pray. You might get what you ask for.

One further Scripture rounds out the lesson. Matthew 7:7-11 is the passage. Ordinarily we concentrate on the first part, in which Jesus promises:

> Ask and it will be given to you; seek and you will find; knock and the door will be opened to you. For everyone who asks receives; he who seeks finds; and to him who knocks, the door will be opened.

We need the rest of it, though:

> Which of you, if his son asks for bread, will give him a stone? Or if he asks for a fish, will give him a snake? If you, then, though you are evil, know how to give good gifts to your children, how much more will your Father in heaven give good gifts to those who ask him!

No, the Lord's arm is not too short, but our patience often is. Our heavenly Father doesn't want to give us bad gifts, but good.

Remember my friend whose conversation with God I quoted at the beginning of the chapter? Let me quote him once more, this time from a letter he wrote just two months later. He reports progress on all fronts. The lawsuit is still pending, but he has found he can live with the uncertainties of it. He is now trusting that there will be money for his daughter's wedding and gift. He has completed one of the best business trips he has ever had, and his business has picked up enough that he has already added staff. His prayer to God now includes these thoughts:

> The most important aspect of all that has happened over the past two months is that I've learned that some of these previously unsolvable situations were, in fact, solvable. Once I turned them

over to You, Lord, the solutions turned out to be much better (and easier) than any I could think of by myself. Some of the more serious problems were solved by occurrences totally beyond my control. Another important point is the things that have not yet concluded no longer cost me personal energy and motion. I trust that whatever the outcome may be, it will be according to what You want and You will see me through to a successful conclusion.

Thank You, Lord. I will try to trust You—always!

So will I.

Chapter 13

When Death Comes Anyway

John 11:17-27

"Everything is possible for him who believes" (Mark 9:23). Victory in Jesus.

"Have faith in God. . . . I tell you the truth, if anyone says to this mountain, 'Go, throw yourself into the sea,' and does not doubt in his heart but believes that what he says will happen, it will be done for him. Therefore I tell you, whatever you ask for in prayer, believe that you have received it, and it will be yours" (Mark 11:22-24).

Victory in Jesus.

"Ask and it will be given to you; seek and you will find; knock and the door will be opened to you. For everyone who asks receives; he who seeks finds; and to him who knocks, the door will be opened" (Matthew 7:7-11).

Victory in Jesus.

"If you have faith as small as a mustard seed, you can say to this mulberry tree, 'Be uprooted and planted in the sea,' and it will obey you" (Luke 17:6).

Victory in Jesus.

"And I will do whatever you ask in my name, so that the Son may bring glory to the Father. You may ask me for

anything in my name, and I will do it" (John 14:13, 14).
Anything, Lord?
"Anything."
Then don't let _____ die!
Victory in Jesus. Does that mean victory over the final
enemy, death? But what about when your loved one dies any-
way, in spite of your faith, in spite of your prayers? Do you
call that victory?

Throughout the writing of this book, these questions
have never left my mind. Joy and I prayed and believed and
trusted, but Lane died anyway. For months afterward, the
questions would not leave us alone. Jesus' promises, the ones
quoted above, rang in our ears. They rang hollow.

We didn't go as far in our protesting as David Biebel did
when his second son became afflicted with the neurological
disease which claimed his firstborn son in early childhood.
Biebel, an evangelical pastor, cried out in his "Lament,"

Destroy! Destroy! Our little boy,
What sad, demented mind, unkind
Would dare?
GOD?

The day he learned of the diagnosis, he couldn't restrain his
honest feelings. "If that's the way it's going to be, then God
can go to Hell!" Driving to his parents' home that night to tell
them Christopher now had the illness that took Jonathan's
life, he reflected some more on his blasphemous outburst.
Then he realized what he had said. That's what Good Friday is
all about, he told himself. On Golgotha, the place of the skull,
God *did* go to Hell. He then comprehended God's message:

"I understand, my son. I've been there already. I've felt your
pain and carried your sorrows. I know your words arose from
grief beyond control and I love you still and always will."[1]

Our comfort came from another instance in Jesus' life. In
our sorrow we identified with Martha, Jesus' good friend. She
was as puzzled by the Lord's behavior as we were. Thinking
through the verses of John 11 helped us. We needed to hear
what Jesus told Martha and Mary.

The sisters had sent word of their brother Lazarus's serious illness. They knew Jesus would come immediately, since He and Lazarus were so close. But Jesus didn't come. According to John, he deliberately waited, postponing his arrival in Bethany until Lazarus had already been in the tomb four days. This time there wasn't going to be victory in Jesus for Mary and Martha.

The fourth day is significant. The Jews believed that after death the soul hovered over the body for that long before departing. Jesus apparently wanted everyone to be certain that Lazarus hadn't merely swooned or was in a coma before rescuing him. He was dead.

Faith in Jesus' ability to heal

"Lord," Martha said to Jesus, "if you had been here, my brother would not have died. "

Victory over the illness would have been possible, if only Jesus had arrived on time, Martha believes. She has complete faith in Jesus' power to heal the sick. Her words confess her faith. But they also contain disappointment. "You weren't here, so he died." And accusation. "Why didn't You come sooner?"

Joy and I expressed them all, faith, disappointment, and accusation.

"Lord, why did You let this happen?

"Lord, we prayed to You faithfully every day for our children. 'Please take care of them, Lord,' we asked You without fail. Why did You let this happen?

Have you also sometimes sounded like Martha?

"Lord, day and night I've been doing everything I could for my loved one. Night and day I prayed for healing. I trusted You. Why did You let this happen? Why couldn't You have saved her?

"If only You had been here, if only You had answered our prayers, this would not have happened."

Such questions and complaints are grounded in faith. You don't scold someone who doesn't exist. You don't chastise someone for not doing what He doesn't have the power to do. Martha believes. "You could have saved Lazarus, Jesus, if only You had come sooner."

Belief in life after death

"But I know that even now God will give you whatever you ask."
Jesus said to her, "Your brother will rise again."
Martha answered, "I know he will rise again in the resurrection at
the last day."

Like many of her countrymen, Martha believed in a resurrection from the dead, not totally unlike our modern opinion. In recent years there has been a resurgence of faith in life after death, not exactly the resurrection of the dead the Jews believed in, but a kind of immortality of the soul. It's often a groundless belief in belief. At funeral services people are sometimes embarrassing when they utter their rather desperate clichés claiming immortality for the deceased. Theirs is more a hope against hope than a reasoned conviction borne of a close walk with God. Without scriptural foundation and without any evidence that the deceased had any relationship with God, they take over the pastor's job and preach the dearly departed into Heaven.

A prayer from the Common Book of Prayer captures this general mood of hopefulness in the face of death: "O Lord, support us all the day long, until the shadows lengthen, and the evening comes, and the busy world is hushed, and the fever of life is over, and our work is done. Then in thy mercy, grant us a safe lodging, and a holy rest, and peace at the last."[2] What is desired in life after death is peace and rest and safe lodging in the bosom of the Father, regardless of the kind of life lived on earth. Martha, who has already given up Lazarus, is satisfied that his new existence is a safe and restful one until the final resurrection.

Trust in Jesus' authority over life and death

Jesus said to her, "I am the resurrection and the life. He who believes in me will live, even though he dies; and whoever lives and believes in me will never die. Do you believe this?"

What Jesus has in mind is something quite different from a vague, other-worldly immortality that we somehow enter when we leave this earth. In fact, He directs Martha's attention from death and the afterlife to himself. The critical consideration here is not the transition from life to death to life after death, but a saving relationship with the One through whom we make the transition. "He who believes in me will live, even though he dies."

The frank realism of this conversation is impressive, especially to someone still smarting from the sting of loss. Both Martha and Jesus speak matter-of-factly about life and death. No euphemisms, no beating around the bush. Our own culture is more guarded. Death has replaced sex as the ultimate taboo. We can't talk about it. Even as recently as my childhood, talk of death entered as a matter of natural course into polite conversations, but sex was spoken of only indirectly, with plenty of protective circumlocutions. Now we feel at liberty to say or display anything sexual.

While sensual bodies are flaunted, however, dead ones are discreetly hidden beneath sheets, under coffin lids, away from the children. A flourishing industry has arisen to protect us from the awfulness of death, to bring dignity to the dying process, and to prolong that dying as long as inhumanly possible. Death is to be delayed at all costs. Let the doctor practice his magic in the hospital room—but keep the minister away lest someone get the idea that the patient is about to leave this earth. Death is taboo.

But not for Martha and Jesus, who can talk honestly because they are not without hope.

"He who believes in me will live, even though he dies; and whoever lives and believes in me will never die."

That is, not ultimately. Death doesn't have the last word. There is more to life than flesh and blood. The body will be laid aside, but the person outlasts the body. What is of the earth will be at last consigned to the earth, yet there's more to the person than earth can hold.

"Do you believe this?"

"Yes, Lord," she told him, "I believe that you are the Christ, the Son of God, who was to come into the world."

Martha is beginning to catch on, but she doesn't grasp the full significance of His words, as we will learn a little later. Because she trusts Him, though, she's going to see some miraculous things.

Her perplexity is understandable. When death hits, as I said earlier, a barrage of questions hit you. You find yourself raising issues that haven't bothered you before, and harboring doubts and welcoming guilt that nearly maddens you. "Oh, if only I had done this, if only I had said that, if only, if only." As if *you* held the key of life and death for this person.

When Christians claim Jesus as Lord of life and Lord of death, we are acknowledging our personal powerlessness; we don't have any authority over life and death. He is Lord, not we. Guilt eases when we admit this truth. "The Lord gave, and the Lord hath taken away; blessed be the name of the Lord" (Job 1:21, *King James Version*). This is not a scriptural platitude for us. It's reality.

How this God-centered philosophy of life works is described by James Dobson in his recounting of a television documentary on dying. The producer had obtained permission from a cancer specialist to place cameras in his clinic, where he captured three patients on film, two men and a woman, from the moment they learned they had cancer to the end of their ordeal. The camera recorded their initial shock and disbelief and their subsequent fear and anger. Two of the patients apparently had no faith in God; they reacted with great anger and bitterness. They appeared to fight their disease and everybody else who was trying to help them cope with its ravages. Their personal relationships, including their marriages, were shaken.

The third patient was a black preacher in his late sixties. When he was told, he didn't panic. He quietly raised some questions, thanked the doctor for his concern and left the clinic. The cameras followed. He and his wife stopped beside their old car to pray. In succeeding months he never lost his poise nor became glib. He gave every evidence of his belief that the Lord was in control.

The cameras were also present when he delivered his last sermon. Dobson recorded part of it.

> Some of you have asked me if I'm mad at God for this disease that has taken over my body. I'll tell you honestly that I have nothing but love in my heart for my Lord. He didn't do this to me. We live in a sinful world where sickness and death are the curse man

has brought upon himself. And I'm going to a better place where there will be no more tears, no suffering, and no heartache. So don't feel bad for me. Besides, our Lord suffered and died for our sins. Why should I not share in His suffering?

Then he began to sing, without accompaniment, in an old, broken voice:

> Must Jesus bear the cross alone,
>   And all the world go free?
> No; there's a cross for everyone,
>   And there's a cross for me.
>
> How happy are the saints above,
>   Who once went sorrowing here!
> But now they taste unmingled love,
>   And joy without a tear.
>
> The consecrated cross I'll bear,
>   Till death shall set me free,
> And then go home my crown to wear,
>   For there's a crown for me.

A few days later he died.[3]

As I've confessed earlier on these pages, we've had our share of ups and downs at our house. This last *down,* our son's death, was the worst, but a long time ago we embraced some truths that have guided our ministry. You can't be in pastoral work—you really can't even be in the church—for too long without suffering with your fellow members of the body. When you are in Christ, you can't really expect, can you, not to share the pain of the world He died for? If Christ is in you and you are in Him, you can't separate yourself from the business of the suffering Lord. He endured a crucifixion. He promised that His true disciples would also take up their crosses in order to follow Him. We really can't escape. If you love, you will suffer because of it. You will do so willingly, although not always in ways you might have predicted. If you understand that heartache on behalf of the beloved is intrinsic to love itself, then you grasp why Jesus had to die, and why He took such pains to help His friends Martha and Mary deal with the death of Lazarus before He brought Lazarus out of the tomb. He could call Lazarus out of his burial place this time, but He could not kill death. Where there's life there will be death. But where there is death there can also be victory. It is possible to survive the trauma—and it isn't by being given answers to all our questions, explanations for all our dilemmas. It's by accepting the final decision of Him who has authority over life and death and trusting in the grace of the sovereign Lord.

In the weeks following our son's death, hundreds of people came to our side. Some of our friends with the best of intentions preached sermonettes, wanting to infuse us with their faith. Their preachments didn't help much. Words flowed easily from the lips of people who hadn't stood where we were standing. Their meaning was accurate, but advice offered too easily does not penetrate deeply. We were most consoled by others who also have loved and lost. They talked little but said much. You get through life's heaviest, hardest crises not with explanations but with companions.

Jesus offers His personal company here—"I am the resurrection . . ."—as earlier He had told His disciples, "I am the way . . . ."

Gratitude for Jesus' tears

I have confessed elsewhere how I committed sacrilege in our high school youth group. From time to time we were asked to answer roll call with a memorized Scripture. A couple of us thought we were very clever. "'Jesus wept,' John 11:35," we blurted out. The shortest verse in the Bible.

I have to tell you what this means to me now.

"Where have you laid him?" Jesus asked.

"Come and see, Lord," they replied.

Jesus wept.

Then the Jews said, "See how he loved him!"

After the memorial service for our son, one of the men in our choir, a big guy, walked up and embraced me. He started to say something, couldn't get it out, sobbed, and walked away. I'll never forget that moment.

Now when I read, "Jesus wept," in those two words I hear:

"For God so loved the world, that *he gave his one and only Son,* that whoever believes in him shall not perish but have eternal life."

Through Jesus' tears, I can grasp something of the love of God. When you're walking through the valley of the shadow of death, you don't need explanations or advice or people's well-intentioned condescension. What keeps you from despair are the tears of those who have been there and survived and who will walk with you through the night.

"I am the resurrection and the life. He who believes in me will live, even though he dies; and whoever lives and believes in me will never die. Do you believe this?"

"Yes, Lord, . . . I believe you are the Christ, the Son of God, who was to come into the world."

Yes, Lord, I believe You are the one who gave Your life that we might live. Yes, Lord, I believe You understand. Yes, Lord, I believe You will accompany me through this horror and that, because of You, death will not defeat me.

But some of them said, "Could not he who opened the eyes of the blind man have kept this man from dying?"

Yes, He could have, but He chose not to. Commentators usually point out that by delaying, Jesus was able to perform this resurrection miracle. If He had come sooner, He could have healed Lazarus but not raised him from the dead. Jesus had this larger lesson to teach, so He waited.

They are right, of course, but perhaps Jesus waited for another reason. He wanted to help the sisters increase their faith, to give insight into the mutual ministry of mourning. He wanted them—and us—to know about the tears of God who does not abandon us to face life's greatest extremity alone.

That's victory in Jesus.

Endnotes

Chapter 1, For the Time of Your Life

[1]Clifton Fadiman, *The Treasure of the Encyclopaedia Britannica*. New York: Viking Penguin, 1992, p. 562.

[2]Quoted in Stephen Bates, *If No News, Send Rumors*. New York: St. Martin's Press, 1989, p. 14.

Chapter 2, Let the Lord Be the Lord!

[1]Henry Adams, *The Education of Henry Adams*. Boston: Houghton Mifflin Company, 1946, pp. 12-14.

[2]Oswald Chambers, *My Utmost for His Highest*. New York: Dodd, Mead and Company, 1935, p. 47.

[3]Hans Küng, *Credo*. New York, et al: Doubleday, 1992, p. 11.

[4]Corrie ten Boom, *Each New Day*. Old Tappan, New Jersey: Fleming H. Revell Co., 1977, p. 164. Her text is from the *Revised Standard Version*.

Chapter 3, Why Love Is Not Enough

[1]In "Frederick Buechner and the Literature of Grace," by Nancy Myers, in *Mission Journal,* May 1981, p. 23.

[2]Louis Kronenberger, *Aphorisms,* p. 324.

[3]Quoted in James W. Fowler, *Stages of Faith.* San Francisco: Harper and Row, 1981, p. 161.

[4]Robert McAfee Brown, *Is Faith Obsolete?* Philadelphia: The Westminster Press, 1974, p. 107.

[5]*A Window to Heaven.* Grand Rapids: Zondervan Publishing House, 1992, p. 23.

[6]Elton Trueblood, "The Center of Certitude," *Faculty Dialogue,* Winter 1992. Portland, Institute for Christian Leadership, p. 2.

[7]*A New Far Glory: The Quest for Faith in an Age of Credulity.* Quoted in Martin E. Marty, *Context,* August 15, 1993, p. 6.

[8]Philip Yancey, *Disappointment with God.* Grand Rapids: Zondervan Publishing House, 1988, pp. 252-253.

Chapter 4, The Great Breakthrough:Gratitude

[1]Garry Wills, *Reagan's America: Innocents at Home.* Garden City, New York: Doubleday and Company, 1987, p. 33.

[2]Robert Fulghum, *All I Really Need to Know I Learned in Kindergarten.* New York: Villard Books, 1986, p. 153-155.

[3]Eugene Lyons, *Herbert Hoover, a Biography.* Garden City, New York: Doubleday and Company, 1964, pp. 29, 30.

Chapter 5, When the Coach Needs Coaching

[1]Matthew Simpson, *Lectures on Preaching.* New York: Phillips and Hunt, 1879, p. 166.

[2]William Barclay, *The Daily Study Bible: The Acts of the Apostles.* Philadelphia: The Westminster Press from The Saint Andrew Press, Second Edition, December 1955, p. 151.

[3]In his Introduction to *The Incarnation of the Word of God* (Macmillan, 1947).

[4]*Forbes,* May 25, 1992, p. 316.

[5]In "Fyodor Dostoevsky: God and Passion," by Eugene H.

Peterson, in *Reality and the Vision,* ed. Philip Yancey. Dallas, et al: Word Publishing, 1990, p. 19. [Italics mine].

6Quoted by E. Ray Jones in his address at the North American Christian Convention in Louisville, Kentucky, July 7, 1989.

7*Forbes,* May 25, 1992, p. 316.

8Ronald W. Clark, *Einstein, the Life and Times.* New York and Cleveland: World Publishing Company, 1971, p. 416.

9R. C. Sproul, John Gerstner and Arthur Lindsley, *Classical Apologetics.* Grand Rapids: Academie Books, Zondervan, 1984, pp. 69. 70.

10"The Reviewing Business," *A Treasury of American Writers from Harper's Magazine,* ed. Horace Knowles. New York: Bonanza Books, 1985, p. 261.

11*A Life in Our Times.* New York [or Boston]: Houghton Mifflin Company, 1981 p. 31.

Chapter 6, How Can I Know What God Wants?

1William Barclay, *Testament of Faith.* London and Oxford: Mowbrays, 1975, p. 89.

2*Reality and the Vision,* ed. Philip Yancey. Dallas, et al: Word Publishing, 1990, p. xii.

3*Surprise Endings.* Sisters, Oregon: Multnomah Press, 1993, pp. 116-118.

4Paul Wilson, *Disturbing the Peace.* New York: Alfred A. Knopf, 1990, p. xv.

5Mildred Welshimer Phillips, *Addresses,* pp. 42, 43.

Chapter 7, Why Does It Take So Long to Get It Right?

1October 18, 1993. By Dan Friday.

2A. T. Pierson, *George Mueller of Bristol.* Revel Company, p. 134.

3"The Rainy Day," 1842.

4Larry King, *Tell It to the King.* New York: G. P. Putnam's Sons, 1988, p. 111.

5Robert J. Morgan, "What Dolly Parton Did for My Ministry," *Leadership Magazine,* Winter 1994, p. 86.

[6]M. Scott Peck, M.D., *A World Waiting to be Born.* New York, et al: Bantam Books, 1993, p. 104.

Chapter 8, Casting Off Every Weight

[1]*Christianity Today,* February 10, 1992, p. 38.

[2]I borrowed this version of the story from Bob Russell, *Making Things Happen,* Standard Publishing, 1987, p. 197. I don't know where he got it.

[3]*Toxic Parents.* New York, et al: Bantam Books, 1989, p. 188.

[4]*Reflections on the Psalms.* New York: Harcourt, Brace and World, Inc., 1958, p. 25.

[5]Quoted by Matthew Arnold. *Matthew Arnold, Poetry and Prose,* ed. John Bryson. Cambridge, Mass: Harvard University Press, 449-50.

[6]Tony Campolo, *How to be Pentecostal without Speaking in Tongues.* Dallas, et al: Word Publishing, 1991, p. 92.

[7]John M. Krumm, *The Art of Being a Sinner.* New York: Seabury Press, 1967, p. 100.

[8]M. Scott Peck, *Further Along the Road Less Traveled.* New York, et al: Simon and Schuster, 1993, p. 46.

[9]*The Arizona Republic,* Saturday, June 16, 1984, p. A3.

[10]*The Arizona Republic,* November 25, 1988, p. 17.

[11]Quoted in William H. Calvin, *The Cerebral Symphony.* New York, et al: Bantam Books, 1989, p. 162.

[12]Norman Vincent Peale, *You Can Have God's Help with Daily Problems.* Pauling, New York: Foundation for Christian Living, 1980, p. 151.

Chapter 9, Keep On Keeping On

[1]Barbara W. Tuchman, *The First Salute.* New York: Alfred A. Knopf, 1988, pp. 82, 83.

[2]Barbara W. Tuchman, *The Guns of August.* New York: Bonanza Books, 1982, p. 233.

[3]Margaret T. Applegarth, *Twelve Baskets Full.* New York: Harper and Brothers, 1957, p. 39.

[4]E. Stanley Jones, *The Way to Power and Poise*. New York and Nashville: Abingdon-Cokesbury Press, 1949, p. 158.

[5]Quoted by Harry Emerson Fosdick, *Real Person,* p. 225.

[6]Charles Barkley, *Outrageous.* p. 168.

[7]Robert Coles, *The Call of Service.* Quoted in *Context,* March 15, 1994, pp. 3, 4.

[8]Quoted in Elton Trueblood, *Alternative to Futility.* Harper and Brothers, 1948, p. (Ch. IV).

Chapter 10, Remember Who You Are and What You Have

[1]From Bonhoeffer's manuscript *Temptation,* quoted by Charles R. Swindoll in *Three Steps Forward Two Steps Back.* Bantam Books, 1980, p. 99.

[2]*The Wisdom of the Saints,* ed. Jill Haak Adels. New York, Oxford: Oxford Press, 1987, p. 151.

[3]William Barclay, *Testament of Faith.* London and Oxford: Mowbrays, 1975, p. 44.

[4]Page 45.

[5]*The Wisdom of the Saints,* ed. Jill Haak Adels. New York, Oxford: Oxford Press, 1987, p. 151.

[6]*The Habit of Being,* Letters of Flannery O'Connor, ed. Sally Fitzgerald. New York: Vintage Books, 1979, p. 258.

[7]*The Business of Heaven (Daily Readings from C. S. Lewis),* ed. Walter Hooper. Great Britain: Collins Fount Paperbacks, 1984, p. 17.

[8]Arthur Miller, *Time Bends.* New York: Grove Press, 1987, p. 425.

[9]J. Wallace Hamilton, *Serendipity.* Westwood, New Jersey: Fleming H. Revell Company, 1965, p. 34.

[10]Quoted in George Gallup, Jr., and David Poling, *The Search for America's Faith.* Nashville: Parthenon Press, 1980, 104.

[11]*Counterattack.* Portland: Multnomah Press, 1988, p. 29.

[12]Gordon MacDonald, *Rebuilding Your Broken World.* Nashville: Nelson, 1988, pp. 47, 53.

[13]New York: William Morrow and Company, co. 1989, pp. 122, 123.

[14]*Money, Sex and Power.* San Francisco: Harper and Row, 1985, p. 178.

[15]*Disappointment with God.* Grand Rapids, MI: Zondervan Publishing House, 1988, pp. 114-115.

[16]Richard Foster, *Money Sex and Power,* p. 180.

Chapter 11, When You Can't Trust Anybody

[1]*Time,* December 28, 1992, p. 16.

[2]*The God of Stones and Spiders.* Wheaton: Crossway Books, 1900, pp. 20, 21.

[3]Sissela Bok, in Bill Moyers, *A World of Ideas,* ed. Betty Sue Flowers. New York: Doubleday, 1989, p. 239.

[4]*Congregation,* ed. David Rosenberg. San Diego, et al: Harcourt Brace Jovanovich, 1987, pp. 56, 57.

[5]Ted W. Engstrom, *Integrity.* Waco: Word Books, 1987, pp. 45, 46.

Chapter 12, When Everybody Is Complaining

[1]John Killinger, *Christ in the Seasons of Ministry.* Waco: Word Books, 1981, p. 47.

Chapter 13, When Death Comes Anyway

[1]Diane M. Komp, *A Window to Heaven.* Grand Rapids: Zondervan Publishing House, 1992, p. 119.

[2]The Episcopal Church, *The Book of Common Prayer.* September, 1979. New York: The Church Hymnal Corporation.

[3]*Focus on the Family,* September 1993, pp. 3, 4.